"It's Easier than Cheezits!"

D1528722

Joy Bazemore

CONTENTS

    "Don't borrow trouble"

    "You have to go to bed so I can get some rest"

    "I married him for better or worse, but not for lunch"

    "Decide what kind of relationship you want to have in ten years"

    "We're spending your inheritance"

Index of Recipes

Introduction

My mama was a rare mixture of East Texas country girl, committed missionary to the Chinese people, smart Virginia choir director/organist, and fun-loving woman. Her speech followed this pattern. She spoke correct English most of the time, but suddenly, once in awhile, out popped a fragment of Chinese wisdom or some "Texas talk." Her colloquialisms were picturesque and usually right on target (if you knew what on earth she was talking about).

For instance,

> "I'm just telling you how the cow ate the cabbage."
> "It was all cattywhompus."
> "There came a gully washer last night."
> "Don't have a hissy. Get down off your high horse."
> "Cherie doesn't hold a candle to her mother."
> "My hair looks like Ned."
> "Boo bahng, boo mahng!"

Was that "clear as mud"? Maybe I better start at the beginning and do some explaining. While I'm at it, I might find some spiritual lessons in these crazy sayings.

"Yonder"

Recently I read an interesting statement: "If you don't know what *yonder* is, you don't belong in the South." Well, Mama belonged. *Yonder* was one of her favorite words. *Down yonder, up yonder, out yonder, back yonder, over yonder,* and *in yonder.* I'm glad it never became politically incorrect to say *yonder* because Mama would've just died. She would have had to be quiet long before her brain damage occurred.

Some of you (and yes, I'll go ahead and forgive you right now) are wondering what a *yonder* is. It's sort of a place but not a specific place. You can't measure *yonder.* I guess it's rather like a cloud. You can't touch it, but it's there.

The concept and usage of *yonder* would probably not work for a control freak or a neat freak (or a Northerner, as previously stated). For instance, "Put it over yonder" means "Just put it somewhere over there." Major meltdown for a neat freak who thinks everything has a place and must be put in that place or else. I always wondered *or else what?* I have no problem with *yonder* because I am a free spirit when it comes to housekeeping. You can put it over yonder, and if I ever get tired of it being over yonder, I'll move it back yonder or out yonder.

A problem with non-specifics is what makes some people have so much trouble with faith. Faith is "confidence in what we *hope for* and assurance about what we *do not see*" (Hebrews 11:1, my emphasis). Granted, some personality types find hope and the unseen easier to handle than other types do. Some are naturally dreamers and others are planners. Some deal in abstract ideas and others in concrete thoughts. Some are energized by spontaneity while charts, tables, lists, and predictable outcomes invigorate others. Here's the truth, folks. God made us all, diverse though we are. And if our Creator says, "Without faith, it is impossible to please God" (Hebrews 11:6), then we need to fight our own personalities and grab onto the non-specific, yet very real thing called faith. Just do it.

> By faith Noah, when warned about things not yet seen, in holy fear built an ark to save his family. (Hebrews 11:7)

> By faith Abraham, when called to go to a place he would later receive as his inheritance, obeyed and went, even though he did not know where he was going. (Hebrews 11:8)

> By faith Moses, when he had grown up, refused to be known as the son of Pharaoh's daughter. He chose to be mistreated along with the people of God rather than to enjoy the fleeting pleasures of sin. He regarded disgrace for the sake of Christ as of greater value than the treasures of Egypt, because he was looking ahead to his reward. (Hebrews 11:24-26)

Did you notice "holy fear" and "even though" and "chose...because he was looking ahead"? These men weren't indifferent to nerves and uncertainty. They had the same human makeup you and I have. But each put down his fears and doubts and allowed God to place him in a 'yonder' situation.

What about us? What are we going to do? It all comes down to this question: "Who are we going to trust?" I say trust the trustworthy One. Trust the Eternal One. Trust the One who knows. Trust the "same yesterday, today, and forever" One (Hebrews 13:8). Trust the One who is love. Trust the all-powerful "I am with you" One (Isaiah 41:10). Trust Him with your heart and your mind and your circumstances.

Let's take a quick course in *over yonder* and *back yonder*. Over yonder is usually in a closer vicinity than back yonder. Say you're inside the house. Over yonder is in the same room. Back yonder is somewhere else in the house, probably not in the living room, which is the 'front room.' If you're in the back yard, over yonder is still in the back yard, but back yonder is in the woods. So, if you buried the dog over yonder, you might can find the mound somewhere at the edge of the lawn or flower bed, but if you buried it back yonder, you ain't ever gonna find the grave again.

Mama didn't say *back yonder* that much. I think it's because our back yard backed up to another back yard for part of my childhood and backed up to a road the rest of my childhood. And if she was in the house, the bedrooms were *up yonder* or *in yonder*. I hope you're not confused.

Some people have used *back yonder* to describe a non-specific time in the past – "Remember way back yonder when you…?" That's what I'd like to do today.

Trusting God is usually easier the second, third, or fourth time than it is at first. It's probably because we remember back yonder when we trusted Him and He came through. Psalm 136 (verses 3, 10-18,

21-24) is a great example of this:

> Give thanks to the Lord of lords:
> *His love endures forever...*
> to him who struck down the firstborn of Egypt
> *His love endures forever.*
> and brought Israel out from among them
> *His love endures forever.*
> with a mighty hand and outstretched arm;
> *His love endures forever.*
> to him who divided the Red Sea asunder
> *His love endures forever.*
> and brought Israel through the midst of it,
> *His love endures forever.*
> but swept Pharaoh and his army into the Red Sea;
> *His love endures forever.*
> to him who led his people through the wilderness;
> *His love endures forever.*
> to him who struck down great kings,
> *His love endures forever.*
> and killed mighty kings—
> *His love endures forever.*
> and gave their land as an inheritance,
> *His love endures forever.*
> an inheritance to his servant Israel.
> *His love endures forever.*
> He remembered us in our low estate
> *His love endures forever.*
> and freed us from our enemies.
> *His love endures forever.*

They recall that back yonder God delivered them from their foes. As they remember, they feel that they can trust Him to help them again. Then they proclaim, "His love endures forever!"

Take a minute to think back yonder in your life. Has God ever done something for you? Has he provided sustenance? Did He give you comfort at a difficult time? Did He help you find the answer to a dilemma? Were you somehow made aware of His presence when you felt alone? Try to remember the gratefulness and joy you felt at that moment. I dare you to trust now the One who was with you or for you back yonder. I fully believe that if you do, you will experience His enduring love.

Mama was a stay-at-home mom back in the day when most women were. She cooked three meals a day, sewed, did laundry, mended, cleaned house, and raised us kids. I can't count the number of times I heard her say, "Go out yonder and play." And by *out yonder*, she meant out of the house, it doesn't matter where. So we played on the porch, in the yard, in the ditch, in the driveway, in the street, in the neighbors' yards, and in the woods two blocks over.

Ooh, the imagination that *out yonder* fostered. My neighborhood friends and I played "Swing the Statue," "Red Rover," "Green Light, Red Light," "Mother May I?" and other typical lawn games of the 60's. But we also rode our bikes all over playing store, where everyone's driveway was a different store. Our driveway had a little wall on each side over the ditch, so that was the gas station or the Woolworth's lunch counter. In my backyard where it connected to the neighbors', there was a short hill. We conducted fairy school there, and running down that hill was the learning-to-fly part of fairy school. Up at the Fosters' yard, we climbed trees, did plays and even held a "Little Miss Greengate" pageant, using their shed as the stage.

The woods were *way* out yonder, and I'm thinking that's why I still feel sort of thrilled yet scared when I reminisce about those idyllic hours. Forts, espionage, and living off the land like the earliest Americans did were common themes of our play in the woods. We collected boocoodles of acorns for ammunition, food, decorations, you name it. We crunched through the dead leaves and dry twigs, never fearing snakes or other nasty varmints. It was magical out yonder.

I sometimes find my heart yearning for those days of my childhood, and when I consider why, I think what I'm really longing for is the innocence, freedom, uninhibited imagination, security, and genuine friendships. Where have those things gone? Have I gotten into the comfort zone of societal norms? For instance, in our society, impurity is the norm rather than innocence. Instead of freedom, conformity, greed, and idolatry drive us. And would we rather hold on to our jealousy, anger, and pride than seek authentic relationships?

I want to be an *out yonder* Christian. Maybe even a *way out yonder* Christian. Out of that worldly comfort zone. Daring to chase after Jesus no matter where He takes me. Imaginative in using ordinary things to teach extraordinary truths. Content in what God has given me. Cultivating transparency in myself and others. Though it seems bold, it also seems freeing. It seems glorious.

> I pray that the eyes of your heart may be enlightened in order that you may know the hope to which he has called you, the riches of his glorious inheritance in his holy people. (Ephesians 1:18)

੭

You'd think *up yonder* and *down yonder* would be opposites, and mostly they are. *Up yonder* is upstairs, up in the attic, up the road a piece (another southern saying), or up in the sky. *Down yonder* can be downstairs or down the road a piece (the opposite way from *up yonder*), but it doesn't usually apply to down in the cellar or down in the ground. Don't know why, so it probably wouldn't do any good to ask me. But we can discuss it if it's really important to you. Mama mainly used these two to mean upstairs and downstairs or directions on the road, almost always with a point in the direction she meant. Right now is the most I've ever analyzed this. When Mama said it, I just knew what she meant. Kind of like if you know French, you just know what a French person is saying.

I wonder sometimes if people are perplexed by our church talk. They don't know what on earth we're trying to say. Words like *begotten, repentance, sanctification,* and *fellowship* and phrases like *profession of faith, born again, walk the aisle, hedge of protection,* and *bathe it in prayer* are confusing and maybe off-putting to the public. If they already distrust us or think we're exclusive, then our use of this churchy jargon may prolong the misunderstanding and defeat our cause. We need to speak real. Real is a language that the average person understands. Real is truth stated in simple terms with honesty and compassion. Real doesn't push anything down anyone's throat but rather offers a life-giving meal and a fork. In other words, we've got to admit we are imperfect and use language that helps another person make the same admission. So that we will all go up yonder when we die. And by *up yonder*, I mean heaven.

...let us draw near to God with a sincere heart and with the full assurance that faith brings, having our hearts sprinkled to cleanse us from a guilty conscience and having our bodies washed with pure water. Let us hold unswervingly to the hope we profess, for he who promised is faithful. And let us consider how we may spur one another on toward love and good deeds,... (Hebrews 10:22-24)

Always be prepared to give an answer to everyone who asks you to give the reason for the hope that you have. But do this with gentleness and respect,... (1 Peter 3:15)

Unlike my childhood self, I'm not much of an adventurer. The woods give me the willies. Yonder has unknowns I'm not too keen on. I like my den. My chair. My water bottle. But sometimes I find myself wondering about way out yonder - what it will be like when all are bowing at the feet of Jesus. Fellowshipping with believers from every tribe and nation. Soaring, or maybe with our feet still planted on firm ground. When we all will be completely free.

Then I think, *Aren't we supposed to be experiencing that freedom right now?* In their song "This is How it Feels to be Free" Phillips, Craig, and Dean talk about being in a prison of sin. Then they talk about the cross, about chains being broken, about being forgiven and living a life that is more than they could have imagined. About being free, completely free.

Do I forget that Jesus came to bring my freedom? Luke 4:16-21 records Jesus' visit to Nazareth and a very important proclamation.

He went to Nazareth, where he had been brought up, and on the Sabbath day he went into the synagogue, as was his custom. He

16

stood up to read, and the scroll of the prophet Isaiah was handed to him. Unrolling it, he found the place where it is written:

"The Spirit of the Lord is on me,
because he has anointed me
to proclaim good news to the poor.
He has sent me to proclaim freedom for the prisoners
and recovery of sight for the blind,
to set the oppressed free,
to proclaim the year of the Lord's favor." [Isaiah 61:1]

Then he rolled up the scroll, gave it back to the attendant and sat down. The eyes of everyone in the synagogue were fastened on him. He began by saying to them, "Today this scripture is fulfilled in your hearing."

He was anointed (set apart for a spiritual purpose) to proclaim freedom. To set the oppressed free. To make us favored in the Lord's sight. Not at some future date, but now. If we acknowledge that we are sinners who need a Savior and we accept that the Savior is Jesus who died for us, we can be set free from the bondage of sin and guilt. Not at some future date, but now. We can soar in the knowledge of His unending, unfailing, incomparable love. Not at some future date, but now. Not out yonder, but right here, right now.

Each of the following verses says something about what we are right now. Underline the words and think about what that means in your life.

Dear friends, now we are children of God, and what we will be has not yet been made known. But we know that when Christ appears, we shall be like him, for we shall see him as he is. (1 John 3:2)

17

But you are a chosen people, a royal priesthood, a holy nation, God's special possession, that you may declare the praises of him who called you out of darkness into his wonderful light. Once you were not a people, but now you are the people of God; once you had not received mercy, but now you have received mercy. (1 Peter 2:9-10)

Set your minds on things above, not on earthly things. For you died, and your life is now hidden with Christ in God. When Christ, who is your life, appears, then you also will appear with him in glory. (Colossians 3:2-4)

Therefore, since we have been justified through faith, we have peace with God through our Lord Jesus Christ, through whom we have gained access by faith into this grace in which we now stand. And we boast in the hope of the glory of God. (Romans 5:1-2)

Now that God has accepted us because Christ sacrificed his life's blood, we will also be kept safe from God's anger. Even when we were God's enemies, he made peace with us, because his Son died for us. Yet something even greater than friendship is ours. Now that we are at peace with God, we will be saved by his Son's life. And in addition to everything else, we are happy because God sent our Lord Jesus Christ to make peace with us. (Romans 5:9-11, CEV)

Therefore, there is now no condemnation for those who are in Christ Jesus. (Romans 8:1)

So if the Son sets you free, you will be free indeed. (John 8:36)

Not down yonder, not out yonder, not over yonder, not up yonder, but right here, right now, you are free.

All the recipes in this book are from Mama's recipe box. I don't know where Mama got this recipe, but she fixed it every time I came home from wandering "out yonder" (college, jobs, marriage). This chowder tastes like home. Incidentally, my husband hates it. But he hates all cream soups, so take my recommendation, not his!

Corn Chowder

2 slices bacon, diced
1/3 cup chopped onions
¾ cup chopped celery

Fry bacon. Remove to paper towel to drain. Then sauté vegetables in the bacon drippings.

Stir in:
1 cup diced cooked potatoes (I leave these out because I like potato soup, but I don't like potatoes in my corn chowder. Silly, I know.)
2 tsp. salt
1/8 tsp. pepper
1/8 tsp. thyme (optional)
½ cup water

Beat together and add:
2 cups milk
1 large can creamed corn
1 Tbsp. pimentos
1 Tbsp. parsley
fried bacon

Bring chowder to an almost boil; then lower heat and simmer 10 minutes. Serves 4..

20

"Pretty Is as Pretty Does"

I wasn't a beautiful child. I've seen the pictures, so I know. But I was fetching enough for some stranger every now and then to comment, "Aren't you a pretty little thing?" If my mama was present, which she almost always was, she'd hurry to remind me, "Pretty is as pretty does, Joy," bursting my shiny bubble in short order.

Of course, Mama meant that a gleaming smile doesn't make up for grubby words and glossy blond hair couldn't cover up a grimy attitude. But I got the idea she thought piety was pretty and therefore, anything less than perfection in my actions or attitudes deemed me ugly. With those expectations, I knew I maybe could be "pretty" for a minute or two, but I lost all hope of spending an entire day being a "pretty" little girl. As an adult and a mother myself, I understand Mama was trying to curb any pride on my part. She certainly didn't intend to make me give up hope. Mama wanted me to aspire to inner beauty that lasts rather than outer beauty that almost always goes south with age. She hoped that I would grasp the concept of true beauty and cling to the One who bestows it.

Let's listen to Paul on the truth about beauty:

> "What actually took place is this: I tried keeping rules and working my head off to please God, and it didn't work. So I quit being a 'law man' so that I could be God's man. Christ's life showed me how, and enabled me to do it. I identified myself

completely with him. Indeed, I have been crucified with Christ. My ego is no longer central. It is no longer important that I appear righteous before you or have your good opinion, and I am no longer driven to impress God. Christ lives in me. The life you see me living is not 'mine,' but it is lived by faith in the Son of God, who loved me and gave himself for me. I am not going to go back on that. Is it not clear to you that to go back to that old rule-keeping, peer-pleasing religion would be an abandonment of everything personal and free in my relationship with God? I refuse to do that, to repudiate God's grace. If a living relationship with God could come by rule-keeping, then Christ died unnecessarily" (Galatians 2:19-21, The Message).

And Titus 3:4-6 tells us,

"But when the kindness and love of God our Savior appeared, he saved us, not because of righteous things we had done, but because of his mercy. He saved us through the washing of rebirth and renewal by the Holy Spirit, whom he poured out on us generously through Jesus Christ our Savior."

In other words,

"God made him who had no sin to be sin for us, so that in him we might become the righteousness of God" (2 Corinthians 5:21).

The truth is, I am not "pretty" because of what I do, but I am beautiful (completely righteous) because of what Jesus did for me. All day every day. Hallelujah!

❧

Why do my eyes always go to the most expensive things? Put four purses in front of me, and I choose the $195 one. Five pieces of furniture? I choose the $4,000 one. Steaks? I choose the filet mignon. Of course, I'm using the word *choose* loosely, because for me, pretty = ludicrously out of my price range.

I've always liked pretty things. Shiny things. Colorful things. Flowery things. Velvety things. And put them all together? Indescribably beautiful. Like the lush, green countryside of Austria dotted with picturesque villages and filled with thousands of flowers and sweet-faced Brown Swiss cattle. I want to go there right now and experience that beauty. Alas, out of my price range at present. Can you relate?

Hold on to your hats, because there is a valuable, beautiful thing right within our reach.

> One thing I have asked from the Lord, that I shall seek:
> That I may dwell in the house of the Lord all the days of my life,
> To behold the beauty of the Lord
> And to meditate in His temple.
> For in the day of trouble He will conceal me in His tabernacle;
> In the secret place of His tent He will hide me;
> He will lift me up on a rock.
> And now my head will be lifted up above my enemies around me,
> And I will offer in His tent sacrifices with shouts of joy;
> I will sing, yes, I will sing praises to the Lord. (Psalm 27:4-6, NASB)

How lovely is your dwelling place,
   O Lord of hosts!
My soul longs, yes, faints
   for the courts of the Lord;
my heart and flesh sing for joy
   to the living God.
Even the sparrow finds a home,
   and the swallow a nest for herself,
   where she may lay her young,
at your altars, O Lord of hosts,
   my King and my God.
Blessed are those who dwell in your house,
   ever singing your praise…
One day in your temple
   is better than a thousand anywhere else. (Psalm 84:1-4,10
CEV)

God is beautiful. His presence is beautiful. His ways are beautiful. And though some people call Christianity exclusive, the Bible tells us that Jesus said,

> "I am the bread of life. **Whoever** comes to me will never go hungry, and **whoever** believes in me will never be thirsty." (John 6:35, my emphasis)

So often our hunger and thirst are for momentary pleasures and meaningless doohickeys. Let's hunger for God, for His presence, for His protection, for His beauty, and we will be satisfied.

"There is only one pretty child in the world, and
every mother has it." – Chinese proverb

Every mother thinks her child is beautiful. She sometimes will admit that other babies are cute, but hers is the cutest, most bright, most angelic in the world. Every mother except my mother. I can't remember the context, but I firmly recall her telling me that my sister Anne was an ugly baby (Sorry, Anne, if you're reading this). Can you believe that? Thank goodness I wasn't the ugly one or my feelings would definitely be hurt. Because how can an ugly baby turn into anything but an ugly adult, right?

I could get into a lot of trouble here, so I'm just going to use fake names* (Oops! Should have thought of that before I said Anne was ugly). Layla* is a very attractive friend of mine. I've seen some of her baby pictures and let's just say she had to grow into that nose. Greg* is a friend's son whose baby head looked like a banana with eyes. However, he is perfectly acceptable in looks now. No more banana head. Celeste* had the worst case of baby acne you've ever seen, and now her skin is clear although beginning to have some wrinkles. Last, but not least, my dear sister Anne is an extremely pretty woman, both inside and out.

On the other hand, I've seen quite a few really beautiful babies that turned into just-average-in-looks kids and grownups. Yet they were somehow able to lead successful lives. How can that be?

We need to go back to the question *What is beauty?* Plato is attributed with this idea: "Beauty lies in the eyes of the beholder." In other words, different people think different things are beautiful. What is beautiful, in your eyes? Think about it for a minute.

Did you list physical attributes? Mental, spiritual, social, or emotional characteristics? I'll admit that I've been practically knocked over by a set of clear blue eyes and reduced to a puddle on the floor by a man's smile. I've also been won over by humor and brought to my knees by a person who is genuinely chasing after Jesus. One of the most beautiful things to me is a man who is gentle with old people and children. All of God's creation, from a ladybug to a snow-covered mountain peak and everything in between, including the unique and unfathomable riches of the human spirit, has drawn my soul closer to my Creator. That's what beauty does. That's probably why every mother looks at her child and sees beauty. The experience of birth is a spiritual thing. When we look at the creation of a child, we see the Creator, whether we realize it or not.

I want to be beautiful in that way. I want to be the beauty that draws people's souls to the Creator, the Lover of their souls.

> Don't be concerned about the outward beauty that depends on jewelry, or beautiful clothes, or hair arrangement. Be beautiful inside, in your hearts, with the lasting charm of a gentle and quiet spirit that is so precious to God. (1 Peter 3:1-4)

> "God made him who had no sin to be sin for us, so that in him we might become the righteousness of God" (2 Corinthians 5:21).

I am the righteousness of God. Wow. Does that mean I can never sin? No. Does it mean I am perfect? No. Does it mean that I always display His beauty? Unfortunately, no. It means that, since the day I trusted Jesus as my Savior, when God looks at me, He sees me as righteous because the blood of Jesus covers all my sin.

I can share the divine nature, even though I am not perfect yet. Listen

26

to 2 Peter 1:3-9 (CEV).

> We have everything we need to live a life that pleases God. It was all given to us by God's own power, when we learned that he had invited us to share in his wonderful goodness. God made great and marvelous promises, so that his nature would become part of us. Then we could escape our evil desires and the corrupt influences of this world.

> Do your best to improve your faith. You can do this by adding goodness, understanding, self-control, patience, devotion to God, concern for others, and love. If you keep growing in this way, it will show that what you know about our Lord Jesus Christ has made your lives useful and meaningful. But if you don't grow, you are like someone who is nearsighted or blind, and you have forgotten that your past sins are forgiven (my underlining).

Growth is beautiful. Well, maybe not toenail growth or mold growth, but most growth is amazing. A child's growth, a relationship's growth, a tree's growth, a Christian's growth. The bud - a promise of beauty - is beautiful in itself. Every stage has a delight of its own.

The CEV translation above lists the attributes (which I have underlined), but the Holman Christian Standard gives it a little different connotation. It uses the word *supplement*. A supplement is something added to complete or reinforce a thing. Let's envision the growth suggested:

- supplement your faith with goodness,
- supplement your goodness with understanding,

- supplement your understanding with self-control,
- supplement your self-control with patience,
- supplement your patience with devotion to God,
- supplement your devotion to God with concern for others, and
- supplement your concern for others with love.

Sometimes we fail to display the beauty of God because we have faith but no goodness. We are hypocrites. Sometimes we have goodness but no real understanding of the divine nature. We need to study the nature of God and then imitate Him. Of course, then our human tendency might lead us to pride over our goodness, so Peter advises supplementing our understanding with self-control. Do you see where I'm going with this? Do you see how the growth works? Do you see the unfolding of something beautiful?

Are you there yet? I'm not. But the idea is to keep on so that our lives will be "oaks of righteousness, a planting of the Lord for the display of his splendor." (Isaiah 61:3b)

You know what's pretty? A smile. You know what I mean? Though Mama didn't talk much after her brain damage, her smile spoke volumes. It was a window to the joy in her soul. It was a nostalgic reminder of all the smiles she'd ever given me. Her *I'm-so-glad-you're-my-daughter* smile. Her *Go-on-and-try,-you-can-do-it* smile. Her *You-make-me-smile* smile. Her *We're-having-fun-together,-aren't-we?* smile. Her *I-love-you-so* smile. Her *Wow,-I'm-proud-of-you* smile. Every one of these smiles and many more were some of the prettiest sights I've ever seen.

You know what else is pretty? Laughter. I'll never forget the sound of my daddy's hysterical laughter while watching an old sitcom. Or the tinkling laughter of eight-year-old girls enjoying a pajama party. The loud bark of laughter my husband gives himself after a particularly corny joke. My own chuckle while reading a good book. Laughter feels so good that it morphs into beauty.

Smiles and laughter are pretty and pretty simple. But some people are more generous with them than others are. I think it's because they've learned something valuable that my parents taught us kids. You gotta laugh at yourself, quit taking yourself so seriously. Everyone flubs up sometimes. Every person has to adapt to change. Every human being can choose to moan and groan or let go and laugh. Granted, you shouldn't laugh at every situation, and it's very hard to smile in some circumstances. But you can learn to let the grace of God adorn you. Count your blessings. Allow the smile of peace to light your face. Be cheerful. Listen to what God says about being cheerful.

- A happy heart makes the face cheerful. (Proverbs 15:13a)
- The cheerful heart has a continual feast. (Proverbs 15:15b)
- A cheerful heart is good medicine, but a crushed spirit dries up the bones. (Proverbs 17:22)

My cheerful heart is good medicine for me, but it's a booster shot for those around me, too. Smiles and laughter are contagious. Mother Teresa once said, "We shall never know all the good that a simple smile can do." And, conversely, if I walk around always crushed in spirit, always wondering *Why me?*, always getting offended by every little thing and then wearing it on my face, my bones will dry up. My friendships may dry up, too, because who wants to be around someone like that? It isn't pretty. At all.

In 2 Corinthians 9:6-8, Paul is talking to the church about a monetary gift, but read these verses and see if you don't agree that the lesson applies to life in general.

> Remember this: Whoever sows sparingly will also reap sparingly, and whoever sows generously will also reap generously. Each of you should give what you have decided in your heart to give, not reluctantly or under compulsion, for God loves a cheerful giver. And God is able to bless you abundantly, so that in all things at all times, having all that you need, you will abound in every good work.

Turns out that the good work we allow God to do in us and through us is a blessing that brings out the pretty in us. And though God loves us unconditionally, I imagine I see Him smiling. It's that *I-love-a-cheerful-giver* smile.

*Mama noted that this recipe was from Juanita Martin. Once again, I don't know who Juanita was, but I'm very thankful for this recipe. Some people call these 'sand tarts,' but they are unlike any other sand tart I've ever tasted. These pecan balls are pretty on the outside and do not disappoint when you get to the inside. I bet they will become a Christmas favorite at your house like they are at ours, and though 36 cookies sounds like a lot, I also bet you'll end up making a second and maybe third batch before the end of the holidays.

Pecan Balls

(makes 3 dozen)

2 cups all-purpose flour
¼ cup confectioner's sugar
2 cups chopped pecans
½ pound (2 sticks) melted butter
1 tsp. vanilla

Mix first three ingredients. Then add the melted butter and vanilla. The mixture will seem too brittle, but form into walnut-sized balls and place 1-2 inches apart on ungreased cookie sheet. Bake at 275 degrees for 1 hour (Yes, sixty minutes).

While cookies are still warm, roll them in confectioner's sugar several times. Let cool, and then store in airtight container.

"It's Easier than Cheezits!"

Mama fell and hit her head on May 31, 2001. My brother, sister, and I rushed to Richmond, Virginia to be at her bedside and to support Daddy. During the following days, doctors and therapists of all sorts visited Mama and performed physical and mental tests. Mama was suffering from brain trauma, especially in the speech area of her brain.

I remember clearly a therapist asking Mama her name. Mama screwed up her face and thought and thought. Finally, she joyfully blurted out "Fahrenheit!" Immediately, her face fell, bewilderment wiping out the joy. (I must admit I laughed out loud. Nervous laughter. *What was wrong with Mama??*)

Then the therapist asked her to say the first word that came to her mind for each word the therapist said.

> "Nine." "Ten."
> "Up." "Down."
> "Red." "Blue."
> "Saucer." "Cup."
> "Cat." "Cup."
> "Bread." "Cup."

Uh-oh! Something got stuck. And that was all the talking Mama would do that day. The next day she was quieter, and the following even more quiet. The doctors decided to move her to a rehab hospital because, physically, Mama was fine, but she needed speech therapy, occupational therapy, and time.

By this time, I had been gone from my family and job for four days, and there wasn't much I could do for Mama, so I decided to head home. When I went to say good-bye to Mama, I could tell by the look on her face that she knew I was leaving. I began apologizing, and Daddy started rationalizing, "Margaret, I know you're sad that Joy is leaving, but she has to get back to her family. Besides, you are going to be so busy in the next few weeks with all kinds of therapy that you wouldn't have time to visit even if she was here!"

Furrowing her brows in thought and making chewing motions with her mouth, Mama retorted, "It's easier than Cheezits!" (Good ol' me laughed again. I didn't know those were the last words I'd ever hear Mama say.) Of course, she didn't mean those words to come out. I guess what she meant was, "You don't know! Maybe therapy won't be that bad, and I sure *would* make time to visit with my daughter, if she was *here*, because I love her so."

The rest of the story is that Mama began having seizures a couple of days later. They put her on anti-convulsive drugs and then tried different ones and then had to get them regulated for her needs. By the time they had the seizures under control, Mama had quit talking almost completely. She didn't eat. They had to put a feeding tube in. I must say that God was gracious and took her home to heaven on December 31 of that year, ten days after her 79th birthday.

I miss her still. And I wonder about that Cheezits moment. I visited her several times during those following seven months, and I knew from the wide smile she'd give me that she was extremely happy to see me, but she never spoke. I wish I could have had her longer. I wish she could know my sons-in-law and grandchildren. I wish I could apologize for laughing at her struggles, even though my laughter was nervous, not malicious. I wish I could hug her. I wish...

You never know how long you're going to have a loved one. Make sure you don't let stupid stuff drive a wedge between you. Visit her. Tell him you love him. Ask forgiveness. Forgive her. Laugh with him.

> I urge you to live a life worthy of the calling you have received. Be completely humble and gentle; be patient, bearing with one another in love. Make every effort to keep the unity of the Spirit through the bond of peace. (Ephesians 4:1-3)

> Behold, how good and how pleasant it is for brethren to dwell together in unity! (Psalm 133:1)

> Do nothing out of selfish ambition or vain conceit. Rather, in humility value others above yourselves, not looking to your own interests but each of you to the interests of the others. (Philippians 2:3-4)

I have brain damage. It's true, and sweets caused it. Sort of. You see, the Halloween I was fifteen years old, a friend had a spend-the-night party for a bunch of girls, and not only did we eat candy, but we consumed brownies and sundry other desserts as well. It was, now that I think about it, a revolting amount of gooey calories.

The next day, I went sailing for the only time in my life and began to feel sick. Understandably, I thought I was seasick. And sugarsick (a new, necessary word). Late that night, however, I found out it was appendicitis and surgery was the only option. Afterwards, I was

35

SICK. The kind of sick that tears stomach sutures open. When they tell you not to eat or drink for many hours before surgery, there's a very good reason.

Eventually, the doctor ordered an anti-nausea drug called Compazine. We'll never know if it was an allergy to the drug or an accidental double dose, but hours later I was in a coma. During the four days of my coma, water collected on the right temporal area of my brain and caused brain damage.

So I could say that sweets caused my brain damage. Or, I could maybe blame it on sailing. Or surgery. Or sickness. Or suppository (Bet you weren't expecting that "s" word! - but Compazine is a suppository). OR, if my grandmother, who was staying with me that Sunday morning, was correct and they gave me two doses of the medication, I could accuse the nurse/doctor/whoever. It's so human to want to assign fault and to want to get revenge. But no amount of blaming or suing can right the wrong that my brain suffered.

Blaming and suing are our society's favorite pastimes, and it is easy to get caught up in the mantra, "It's my right." The Bible has a good bit to say about this subject. Let's listen for a minute.

> "Do not seek revenge or bear a grudge against anyone among your people, but love your neighbor as yourself. I am the Lord." (Leviticus 19:18)

> If it is possible, as far as it depends on you, live at peace with everyone. Do not take revenge, my dear friends, but leave room for God's wrath, for it is written: "It is mine to avenge; I will repay," says the Lord. (Romans 12:18-19)

> The very fact that you have lawsuits among you means you have

been completely defeated already. Why not rather be wronged? Why not rather be cheated? (1 Corinthians 6:7)

You, therefore, have no excuse, you who pass judgment on someone else, for at whatever point you judge another, you are condemning yourself, because you who pass judgment do the same things. (Romans 2:1)

"Why do you look at the speck of sawdust in your brother's eye and pay no attention to the plank in your own eye? How can you say to your brother, 'Let me take the speck out of your eye,' when all the time there is a plank in your own eye? You hypocrite, first take the plank out of your own eye, and then you will see clearly to remove the speck from your brother's eye." (Matthew 7:3-5)

Jesus was our teacher. When His disciples wanted to learn to pray, He taught them to say, "Forgive us our trespasses as we forgive those who trespass against us." He clarified further: "For if you forgive other people when they sin against you, your heavenly Father will also forgive you. But if you do not forgive others their sins, your Father will not forgive your sins." (Matthew 6:12 and 14)

What's more, Jesus was our example. He laid down His life for cheaters, mistake-makers, scoffers, offenders, criticizers, unbelievers, etc. From the podium of the cross He spoke these selfless words: "Father, forgive them."

What do you need to do right now to lay down a grudge you've held or to make peace with someone? Begin by saying these words aloud, "I forgive him/her."

❧

When Mama fell and her brain was damaged, I never imagined she wouldn't get well. After all, I had sustained brain damage and I'm okay (Well, most of the time). The ironic thing is that when I started having seizures due to my brain damage, Mama was my number one cheerleader. Her heart would break for me when I was almost to the point of getting my driver's license back and then I'd have another seizure and have to wait another year. I admit that stank, but since I didn't have my own car anyway, I lived through it. She prayed and prayed that I would have a "normal" life and be able to do all the things a young woman dreams about – go to college, get married, have children, have a career.

God answered Mama's prayers. I have had a full, blessed life free from seizures, though I continued to take anti-convulsive medication until about three years ago. I have a degree in education and had a great career as a schoolteacher before and after staying home for ten years with my four beautiful daughters, who are grown now. I'm blessed with one tall, dark, and handsome husband, some mighty fine sons-in-law, ten grandchildren, and many funny, godly, dear friends.

However, when my mama died prematurely, it was like I had hit a huge pothole in the great road I was traveling. Now some of you might think, *She lived to be 79. What did you want??* I'll tell you what I wanted. I expected her to live to be 95. Her mother did. Her mother's two sisters did. Her daddy lived to be 87. Let me tell you that when Mama died at barely 79, I felt gypped. Cheated. Wronged. Hurt.

When you're hurt, you feel the need to blame someone, so I blamed God. I built up a grudge against Him in my heart. But that same year,

2001, a ton of other tragedies and challenges took place in our church, in our nation, and in my family, so I found myself putting aside that grudge and holding on to God for dear life, just like Mama would have done. He didn't fail me.

> Your love, Lord, reaches to the heavens, your faithfulness to the skies. (Ps. 36:5)

> Who is like you, Lord God Almighty? You, Lord, are mighty, and your faithfulness surrounds you. (Ps. 89:8)

> Not to us, Lord, not to us but to your name be the glory, because of your love and faithfulness. (Ps. 115:1)

> But you, Lord, are a compassionate and gracious God, slow to anger, abounding in love and faithfulness. (Ps. 86:15)

His faithfulness is big enough, mighty enough, glorious enough, lasting enough, enough. Are you blaming God for something today? Give up your grudge and hold on to Him. He is faithful.

John 3:16 is the first Bible verse I ever memorized. How about you? Did you learn it in the King James Version like I did? *For God so loved the world, that he gave his only begotten Son, that whosoever believeth in him should not perish, but have everlasting life.*

Through the years I've often picked certain words from that verse and thought about what they mean. *Loved. The world. Only Son. Whosoever. Everlasting life.* Today the word *so* is standing out. God *so* loved.

Study the following synonyms for *so.* Substitute them in the phrase

God so loved.

truly	thoroughly	exceedingly
seriously	deeply	wholly
significantly	to the highest degree	

1 John 4:8 says, "God is love." His whole makeup is love. Every action He takes is from who He is – love.

He desires relationship with us because of love.

He gave Jesus because of love.

He says "No" because of love.

He gives blessing because of love.

He works in disappointment for our good because of love.

He plans our futures with love.

And not just the "Cheezits" kind of love we understand, as wonderful as that human love is, but the *so* kind of love mentioned above that we can't really comprehend. He loves us *so*.

As hard as Mama's death was to accept, once I let go of my grudge, I was able to be thankful for her life, for her legacy, for her faith, even for her death. She wouldn't have wanted to live on in that condition. She would have wanted to see Jesus face to face. She would have wanted to understand fully that love ("For now we see only a reflection as in a mirror; then we shall see face to face. Now I know in part; then I shall know fully, even as I am fully known." (1 Corinthians 13:12)

Can't we trust Him to time things through the lens of perfect love? Can't we agree that the difficulties we may be facing are being allowed because of His love? Shouldn't we praise Him for His love shown through each moment of every day we are alive?

He loves us so.

꙳

Cheezits. I don't know about "easier than," but I know they're delicious. (And I know they are actually called Cheez-it.) The original and white cheddar. Mmm. I want some right now. How about you? And if you get up and go buy a box, will you be disappointed? No! They will taste just like the last ones you had. You can count on Cheezits to meet your high expectations.

Here's a question. What are your expectations of Jesus? Think about it. Maybe even jot a few down.

Why do you expect these things from Him?

Have you ever been disappointed because of one of these expectations?

Our former pastor once said that the reason some people are bitter at God is that they expected God to do something He never promised to do.

Here is an incomplete list of things God promises. I have highlighted some of the words to emphasize the actions we have to take in order to receive these promises.

1. God promises to ease your burdens.

- The burden of sin and death:

  a. **Believe in** the Lord Jesus, and you will be saved. (Acts 16:31)

  b. But to all who **believed** him and **accepted** him, he gave the right to become children of God. (John 1:12, NLT)

- The burdens of life:

  a. "**Come to me**, all you who are weary and burdened, and I will give you rest. (Matthew 11:28)

  b. **Don't worry** about anything; instead, **pray** about everything. Tell God what you need, and **thank him** for all he has done. Then you will experience God's peace, which exceeds anything we can understand. His peace will guard your hearts and minds as you live in Christ Jesus. (Phil. 4:6-7, NLT)

  c. My God will meet all your **needs** according to the riches of his glory in Christ Jesus. (Phil. 4:19)

2. God promises to be with you and strengthen you.

   - The Lord himself goes before you and will be with you; he will never leave you nor forsake you. **Do not be afraid; do not be discouraged**. (Deut. 31:8)

   - He gives strength to the weary and increases the power of the weak. Even youths grow tired and weary, and young men stumble and fall; but those who **hope in the Lord** will renew their strength. They will soar on wings like eagles; they will run and not grow weary, they will walk and not be faint. (Isaiah 40:29)

- "My grace is sufficient for you, for my power is made perfect in weakness." (2 Corinthians 12:9)

3. God promises to teach you.

- I will instruct you and teach you in the way you should go; I will counsel you with my loving eye on you. (Psalm 32:8)

- Whether you turn to the right or to the left, your ears will hear a voice behind you, saying, "This is the way; walk in it." (Isaiah 30:21)

- 'Call to me and I will answer you and tell you great and unsearchable things you do not know.' (Jeremiah 33:3)

4. God promises that He will work in all things for your good if you love Him and trust Him.

- And we know that God causes all things to work together for good to those who love God, to those who are called according to *His* purpose. (Romans 8:28, NAS)

5. God promises to hear and answer prayer.

- The **earnest *prayer*** of a righteous person has great

power and produces wonderful results. (James 5:16, NLT)

- This is the confidence we have in approaching God: that if we **ask anything according to his will**, he hears us. (1 John 5:14)

How does this list compare with the one you jotted down?

What expectations do you have for yourself, considering these verses?

We so easily depend on Cheezits to deliver the same goodness every time. Why should it be hard to count on our Almighty God to always be the same, always act in love, always have our best interests at heart, always provide for our needs? Shouldn't it be easier than Cheezits?

*Recipe from B. Myers (one of Mama's missionary colleagues, I think)

Squash Casserole

2 cups cooked yellow squash (about 1 ½ pounds fresh)
¾ stick butter, melted
2 eggs, beaten
1 tsp. salt
½ tsp. pepper
1 cup chopped onion
1 cup grated cheese
1 cup evaporated milk
2 cups crumbled Cheezits, divided (1 ½ cups, ½ cup)

Mash cooked squash and add all other ingredients except ½ cup crumbled Cheezits.

Pour into greased 2-quart dish and top with remaining ½ cup Cheezits. Bake at 375 degrees for about 40 minutes.

"Kissing Leads to Other Things"

Yes, it does. It's a fact of life. Mama started giving me this warning when I started thinking boys were cute and maybe not too cootie-laden. I was probably about eleven years old and didn't know what "other things" she was talking about because back in my preteen days we were much more innocent than kids are today.

About a year later my friend Jeanie shared the basic facts of life with me, and I told her my parents would *never* have done *that*! Furthermore, I was *never* going to do *that*. Then, when I was fourteen, a boy kissed me, *really* kissed me, and over the next few years I began to realize that the desire growing in me could lead to *that*. So I finally understood why a girl might want to be careful about kissing.

There's no verse in the Bible that says, "God created cause and effect and saw that it was good." But if you search the Scriptures and live life for a day or two, you will find that God created cause and effect. Certain things really do lead to certain other things. Remember last week when I said everything is better with praise and adoration? Well, the reason it's better is because God has ordained that praising Him leads to peace. It absolutely does. So be warned. If you start praising the Lord, you're not going to be able to hang onto the worries that weigh you down or the grudges that grind you down.

Do not be anxious about anything, but in every situation, by prayer and petition, **with thanksgiving**, present your requests to God. And the peace of God, which transcends all understanding, will guard your hearts and your minds in Christ Jesus. (Philippians 4:6-7, my emphasis)

I remember my affliction and my wandering, the bitterness and the gall. I well remember them, and my soul is downcast within me. Yet this I call to mind and therefore I have hope: Because of the Lord's great love we are not consumed, for his compassions never fail. They are new every morning; great is your faithfulness. I say to myself, "The Lord is my portion; therefore I will wait for him." The Lord is good to those whose hope is in him, to the one who seeks him. (Lamentations 3:19-23)

The Lord is my shepherd; I lack nothing. He makes me lie down in green pastures, he leads me beside quiet waters, he refreshes my soul. He guides me along the right paths for his name's sake. Even though I walk through the darkest valley, I will fear no evil, for you are with me; your rod and your staff, they comfort me. You prepare a table before me in the presence of my enemies. You anoint my head with oil; my cup overflows. Surely your goodness and love will follow me all the days of my life, and I will dwell in the house of the Lord forever. (Psalm 23)

One of my family members struggles with anxiety at times. Knowing the truth that praise leads to peace, she downloads praise songs onto her phone, and when she's feeling anxious or upset, she turns on the music and sings along. Oh, the ministry of praise to our hearts! Take time to thank the Lord for this miraculous cause and effect.

"Do you want me to kiss it better?" My three-year-old grandchild had fallen on the driveway and skinned his knee. It wasn't a bad boo-boo, but he needed me to notice his pain and encourage him to move on. Since the reassurance of a simple loving kiss is sometimes all it takes, especially when you're little, he ran to me, lifted his leg up to my bent face, and gratefully accepted the tender touch of my lips. Then he scampered up the driveway again like a chipmunk on caffeine.

Do you ever feel little in this big, bad world? Do you feel you have about as much control as a preschooler has? Do you want your pain to be noticed, even if it's a relatively small pain? Would it be nice to have some bit of encouragement to move on? Jesus has "kisses of compassion" for that.

> Cast **all** your anxiety on him because he cares for you. (1 Peter 5:7, my emphasis)

> Cast your cares on the Lord and he will sustain you; he will never let the righteous be shaken. (Psalm 55:22)

> "Therefore I tell you, do not worry about your life, what you will eat or drink; or about your body, what you will wear. Is not life more than food, and the body more than clothes? Look at the birds of the air; they do not sow or reap or store away in barns, and yet your heavenly Father feeds them. Are you not much more valuable than they? (Matthew 6:25-26)

In Matthew 8-9, Jesus heals a leper, two paralytics, several demon-possessed men, a woman with a fever, a woman with a 12-year-long bleeding problem, two blind men, and many others with all kinds of sicknesses. He also raised a dead girl back to life. Whew! Jesus was busy. Why did he work so tirelessly healing people? In most of the cases, it was because people came to Him or called out to Him to heal them or their loved ones. In the case of the woman with the fever, Jesus observed that she was sick and reached out His hand to touch her. Matthew 9:36 says, "When he saw the crowds, he had compassion on them, because they were harassed and helpless, like sheep without a shepherd." Are you feeling harassed and helpless? Jesus has a "kiss of compassion" for that.

Kisses lead to other things. What did Jesus' compassion for the crowds lead to? In his gospel, Mark tells us, "So He began teaching them many things" (Mark 6:34). Jesus wants to teach us many things to relieve our pain, suffering, embarrassment, harassment, whatever our big or little "boo-boos" are. Let's dig into His Word, and He will tell us marvelous things. Listen to Psalm 119:33-40 (The Message):

> God, teach me lessons for living so I can stay the course.
>
> Give me insight so I can do what you tell me — my whole life one long, obedient response.
>
> Guide me down the road of your commandments; I love traveling this freeway!
>
> Give me a bent for your words of wisdom, and not for piling up loot.
>
> Divert my eyes from toys and trinkets, invigorate me on the pilgrim way.
>
> Affirm your promises to me — promises made to all who fear you.
>
> Deflect the harsh words of my critics — but what you say is always so good.

See how hungry I am for your counsel; preserve my life through your righteous ways!

&

When you're a little kid, you might want your boo-boos kissed better. But when you're a bigger kid, kissing leads to wiping off. Grandmothers' kisses, aunts' kisses, various and sundry odd-people-your-parents-know's kisses. Especially the slobbery ones. Yuck! I'm afraid I may even have hurt my mama's feelings a few times when I felt I was too old for her kisses. Just wiped 'em right off.

A kiss is still a kiss. See, you can rub off a kiss, but the sentiment or passion is still there, hanging in the air or maybe soaked into your skin. Your grimace and frantic wiping does not negate the love, adoration, joy, or appreciation that prompted the kiss. No matter how vehemently you want to repulse the gift or the giver, the kiss is already out there.

This same concept surfaces often when Christians don't understand God's forgiveness. They think their dreadful sins can negate what Jesus has done. They believe their sin is powerful enough to wipe out Jesus' sacrifice, when the opposite is true. Jesus' sacrifice is powerful enough to wipe out every sin. And it's already out there.

> Unlike the other high priests, he does not need to offer sacrifices day after day, first for his own sins, and then for the sins of the people. He sacrificed for their sins **once for all** when he offered himself. (Hebrews 7:27, my emphasis)

No measure of horrific sin and no amount of frantic self-degradation can invalidate Jesus' loving sacrifice on our behalf.

Another group of people who try to "wipe off" Jesus' love are those who don't believe in Him. They claim that what He did isn't real. It's almost as if the idea of His death and resurrection offends them like a slobbery kiss on the cheek by a distant relative, so they swipe at it and think it's been removed. But the proof of the claims of Jesus is already out there. His death by crucifixion was witnessed and recorded by many. More importantly, over five hundred people saw Him after His resurrection!

> For what I received I passed on to you as of first importance: that Christ died for our sins according to the Scriptures, that he was buried, that he was raised on the third day according to the Scriptures, and that he appeared to Cephas, and then to the Twelve. After that, he appeared to more than five hundred of the brothers and sisters at the same time, most of whom are still living, though some have fallen asleep. Then he appeared to James, then to all the apostles, and last of all he appeared to me also, as to one abnormally born. (1 Corinthians 15:3-8)

You know those kisses of my mama's that I wiped off? Sometimes she would tease, "Did you just wipe off my kiss, or were you rubbing it in?" and I would insist, "Rubbing it in, Mama, rubbing it in" while rolling my eyes behind her back.

We do not have the power, my friend, by sin or by unbelief, to undo what Jesus has done. The love that prompted His sacrifice is out there. So believe it. Grab it. Rejoice in it. Rub it in.

Evidently, "other things" can happen without kissing. I know this because though people in some cultures don't kiss, the cultures have not become extinct. Not kissing at all, though, seems very sad to me. I enjoy kissing, both romantically and otherwise. In fact, I cannot hold one of my grandchildren without kissing him or her somewhere on the head, neck, or face. Or arm, hand, foot. It is impossible to not kiss them. I would say that holding a grandchild leads to kissing. Sometimes, even when someone else is holding said grandchild, my lips start twitching. It's cause and effect all over again.

I genuinely love my grandchildren, and kissing naturally comes from that love. Here's a newsflash: According to 1 Corinthians 13, genuine love is supposed to lead to other actions, too.

Love is patient.

Why did Paul list this one first when it's one of the hardest ones to do? Patience doesn't come easily. It takes patience to become patient! Just the other day, I was being impatient with the man I supposedly love the most. I remember coming to the end of that day and thinking *I sure have said 'Help me, Jesus' a lot of times today.* And I remember thinking that I had deserved to be impatient. Because, of course, it's all about me, right?

Isn't this why patience is so hard? Because we're basically selfish beings? Paul mentions a little later in the chapter that love is not self-seeking. I'm thinking he should have stated that one first, and he might not have had to mention the others.

Back to patience, though. What actions can I do to show patience? Sometimes walking away from the exasperating situation for a few minutes is the best bet. It gives us time to think about it from the other person's point of view. And even if her point of view is askew, it gives me time to calm down and speak with love.

I'm sure that if we ask Him, the Holy Spirit will help us think of other actions that show patience.

Love is kind.

Show compassion and understanding. Be thoughtful and courteous. As Paul said in Ephesians 4:32, "Be kind and compassionate to one another, forgiving each other, just as in Christ God forgave you."

Love does not envy.

Envy is a bad word. I don't like to use it, so it's easy to say I don't have a problem with envy. But then I go comparing my life to someone else's life, or my husband to someone else's husband, or my body to someone else's body, and it begins to look a lot like envy. So how can I show the actions of not envying? Maybe by not comparing and by not inviting others to compare their lives, husbands, bodies, etc. with mine. And maybe by genuinely rejoicing with those who rejoice.

Love does not boast; it is not proud.

This sounds like more good advice about not comparing ourselves to others. "Comparison is the thief of joy" is quoted often and is very true. It seems that "Comparison is the enemy of love" should be quoted just as often.

Tomorrow we will tackle the rest of 1 Corinthians 13:4-8. In the meantime, I'm going to go work on the patience part.

Love does not dishonor others.

Being kind sort of precludes dishonoring or disrespecting someone, doesn't it? And if we can conquer the envy/comparison/pride enemy, we won't be trying to belittle someone else. So I guess Paul included this one not as duplication but to make sure we got the message.

Love is not self-seeking.

There it is! And Paul explains the concept beautifully in Philippians 2:3-4 (ESV): "Do nothing from selfish ambition or conceit, but in humility count others more significant than yourselves. Let each of you look not only to his own interests, but also to the interests of others."

Love is not easily angered.

This kind of love, the God-kind we're talking about, is slow to anger. If I find myself getting angry easily, getting impatient, or being unkind and disrespectful, then it's definitely a spiritual problem, because the Lord is slow to anger. Moses knew it, the psalmists knew it, and the prophets knew it. Listen:

> The Lord, the Lord, the compassionate and gracious God, slow to anger, abounding in love and faithfulness,... (Ex. 34:6)

> The Lord is slow to anger, abounding in love... (Numbers 14:8)

> But you are a forgiving God, gracious and compassionate, slow to anger and abounding in love. (Neh. 9:17)

> But you, Lord, are a compassionate and gracious God, slow to anger, abounding in love and faithfulness. (Ps. 86:15)

55

The Lord is compassionate and gracious, slow to anger, abounding in love. (Ps. 103:8)

The Lord is gracious and compassionate, slow to anger and rich in love. (Ps. 145:8)

he is gracious and compassionate, slow to anger and abounding in love,... (Joel 2:13)

I knew that you are a gracious and compassionate God, slow to anger and abounding in love... (Jonah 4:2)

The Lord is slow to anger,... (Nahum 1:3)

Notice that in eight out of the nine times the NIV uses the phrase 'slow to anger' to describe God, there is also a phrase about His great love.

Love keeps no record of wrongs.

Don't we love to keep records? I am amazed when watching a sporting event how the commentators can spew statistics about the players or teams from many years back all the way up to the present. Someone was keeping records! And churches are pros at it. We know how many were present, how much money they gave, and how many decisions were made the third Sunday in July of 1983. Just ask us.

Here's the challenge: we've got to draw the line. We need records. They inspire us and remind us of God's goodness. But if we're writing down, even if just emotionally, the times someone has hurt us or cheated us or been less than loving to us, then our hearts can easily be lead into anger, dishonor, unforgiveness, and bitterness.

Love does not delight in evil but rejoices with the truth. It always protects, always trusts, always hopes, always perseveres. Love never fails.

One of my favorite passages is Romans 8:31-39. I challenge you to read it, but for now let me share the juiciest morsels.

- If God is for us, who can be against us? (Love rejoices with the truth, always protects.)

- Who shall separate us from the love of Christ? (Love always hopes, always perseveres.)

- We are more than conquerors through him who loved us (Love never fails.)

Kissing leads to other things. It's a God-ordained fact. And genuine love leads to humble attitudes and care-filled actions. That's God-ordained fact #2.

*I hate to keep including recipes that will make you fat, but when I was looking for something to go with this week's devotions, I couldn't find any with 'kissing' in the title. So I swapped over to looking for a recipe that I could say leads to something and I can tell you that eating this chicken leads to "Yummmm."

I guess Mama got it from Mrs. Sadler, since she calls it "Mrs. Sadler's Chicken." I think I used to know who Mrs. Sadler is, but I can't remember anymore. I will say that it's perfectly legit to shout, "Hooray for Mrs. Sadler" after eating this. Bon appetit!

Mrs. Sadler's Chicken

*All of the notes in parentheses were Mrs. Sadler's

Sear salted chicken (no flour)   (I used breasts and legs of 3 fryers)

Heat oven to 400 degrees. Heat 2 cans cream of mushroom soup, some butter (I used one stick), and pour over chicken. Place in oven (I added two bottles single cream). After about 30 minutes, turn heat to 325 degrees and let cook till tender (about 2 hours in all).

 If that's a little confusing, here's how I would do it:

8-10 chicken breasts
2 cans cream of mushroom soup
½ cup (1 stick) butter
2 cups whipping cream

Preheat oven to 400 degrees. Sear salted chicken (no flour). Remove chicken to 9 x 13 baking dish. Heat mushroom soup and butter until butter is melted. Stir in whipping cream. Pour over chicken. Bake 30 minutes, covered. Turn heat down to 325 degrees and bake 1 – 1 ½ hours more (until chicken is tender). Serve over rice.

"It Takes All Kinds to Make a World"

I've led sort of a sheltered life. That's a strange statement from a woman who as a missionaries' kid traveled all around Asia and some other parts of the world while she was growing up. I guess what I mean is that I was exposed to other cultures and races and religions, but I was protected from what my parents deemed the most dangerous parts of each of those – anything that might influence my belief system.

Some people would claim I was never allowed to think on my own, but I disagree. I remember quite well when I first realized that my parents' faith could not just transfer to me and that I would have to find out if I really believed the claims of Christianity. I began studying the Bible more intently for myself and through the moving of the Holy Spirit found my own personal faith.

Yet, - and I don't enjoy admitting this - I want everyone else's faith to look just like mine. It's like I don't really want them to find their personal faith in Christ. I want all believers to be alike and be just one big, happy, purple Barney "I love you, you love me" family. I would feel much more comfortable if everyone would like the same music, the same style of preaching, the same way of praying, the same dress code, the same methods of discipleship, etc.

Now to what Mama said: "It takes all kinds to make a world." She usually said this after we met someone who dressed kind of strange or expressed herself in an odd sort of way. I guess my mama was being tolerant of other people's idiosyncrasies. That's good. But there's a much deeper, spiritual truth in this saying, too.

Our great, almighty, completely creative God made a universe of diversity. I could go on for pages just about the different kinds of stars (if I knew anything about them). Deserts, tropical rainforests, tundra, beaches, mountains, waving fields of grain, roses, daisies, heather, tumbleweed, goats, elk, panthers, cotton-tailed rabbits, gnats, eagles, trout, whales, coral, hurricanes, tsunamis, earthquakes, hail, snowflakes, helium, oxygen, beta carotene, the circulatory system, the respiratory system, warts. Need I go on? Each of us could write for days on end and not be able to think of or jot down the whole of God's diverse creation.

> When I consider your heavens,
> the work of your fingers, the moon and the stars,
> which you have set in place,
> what is mankind that you are mindful of them,
> human beings that you care for them?
> You have made them a little lower than the angels
> and crowned them with glory and honor.   (Psalm 8:3-5)

If God created different types of stars and various kinds of heavenly orbs and one particular planet that has just the right atmosphere and temperature and tilt and land/water ratio and on and on, each for its own purpose, can He not have created people with just as much diversity and purpose? Yes.

So here's what I must do. I must develop my own relationship with God through Christ Jesus my Savior. I must find His purpose for my life. I must obey commands He's made clear in His Word. I must pay close attention to the issues and people He places on my heart. I must love the Lord my God with all my heart and my neighbor as myself. I must quit looking at others to judge them and start judging my own sin, my own spiritual nearsightedness, my own inability to care about the things God cares about and to be heart-broken about the things that grieve Him. And I must understand that God created every human being and loves each one as much as He loves me. Yes, it takes all kinds to make a world, and it will take all kinds to make a heaven, too.

> After this I looked, and there before me was a great multitude that no one could count, from every nation, tribe, people and language, standing before the throne and before the Lamb. They were wearing white robes and were holding palm branches in their hands. And they cried out in a loud voice: "Salvation belongs to our God, who sits on the throne, and to the Lamb." (Revelation 7:9-10)

When I was little, an Easter basket was small and simple:

- Boiled, dyed eggs (may I please just say, "Yuck"),
- Jelly beans,
- Robin eggs (you know, the malted milk candy-coated things, and may I please just say, "Yum"), and
- Belle of the ball - center of attention - usually tilting a little to its side, the hollow milk chocolate Easter bunny with the creepy candy eyes.

That was all. No Reese's peanut butter eggs, no Nestle Crunch eggs, no Peeps, no Cadbury's Crème eggs, no toys, no technology, no cellophane wrapping, no big bow. Small and simple, yet I was as excited as kids are these days.

The fact is, I was almost as excited just yesterday because I went to Target and all their Easter candy was 50% off. Telling myself the whole time, *Don't do it!,* I bought Russell Stover chocolate marshmallow eggs – the six-pack. Twix eggs – the six-pack. Brach's tiny jelly beans in little boxes – the six-pack. Tiny robin eggs in little milk cartons (for my grandchildren). Peeps – the fifteen-pack. It was somewhat disgraceful but not too expensive, thanks to the 50% off sale.

What was really disgraceful is what I did with some of that candy when I got home. I binged. I had to taste it all (except for the robin eggs – they were for the grandchildren). Here is what I learned. All of it tasted good. Each was a little different, and I must admit I have my favorites, but I won't publish them here. (Don't want to give any particular candy the big head.) You know why all of it was good? The main ingredient was the same: sugar.

It takes all kinds of candy to make an Easter basket these days, and I bet each of you has a favorite. Now, there is one kind I just will not eat. Licorice. Why did God create licorice? He could have left it out of creation, along with snakes, roaches, mosquitos, flies, and liver, in my humble opinion. But some of you out there are yelling, "No, licorice is the best flavor of jelly bean!" Aha! So you're the ones buying those all-black bags of jelly beans. I would like an all-purple or an all-red bag, but No. They gotta make all-black bags for you weirdos. Whatever!

Here is my point. I enjoyed all the candy I bought because there was no licorice. But your basket could have licorice in it if that's what you like. You could have Skittles or Hershey Kisses or Dove chocolates or Oreo eggs. And it would all be called candy because it has sugar. That's what makes it candy. The sugar.

There are all kinds of Christian worship and Christian preachers and Christian seminaries and Christian rituals and Christian books. You don't have to like them all, but if they have the key ingredient – Christ – then they are Christian. (Conversely, if they leave out Jesus, then I don't think we should call them Christian.)

The bottom line is: If they believe that Jesus is the Savior, the only Savior, who was crucified, buried, and raised from the dead for our sins and our resurrection hope, then they are Christian. The person singing praises from her knees on the dirt of an African hut is just as Christian as the woman holding a hymnbook in a Methodist church in Kentucky. The one using slang or stammering sentences to talk to her Jesus from a jail cell is just as Christian as the one repeating the age-old Apostles' Creed in a Presbyterian sanctuary. The young mother hanging on every word about Jesus the pastor in shirt sleeves is preaching is just as Christian as the matriarch who will only listen to a man in a suit. The wrappings and the other ingredients don't matter. You've just got to have the key ingredient – Jesus Christ.

> As Scripture says, "Anyone who believes in him will never be put to shame." For there is no difference between Jew and Gentile—the same Lord is Lord of all and richly blesses all who call on him, for, "Everyone who calls on the name of the Lord will be saved." (Romans 10:11-13)

So in Christ Jesus you are all children of God through faith, for all of you who were baptized into Christ have clothed yourselves with Christ. There is neither Jew nor Gentile, neither slave nor free, nor is there male and female, for you are all one in Christ Jesus. (Galatians 3:26-28)

As Peter entered the house, Cornelius met him and fell at his feet in reverence. But Peter made him get up. "Stand up," he said, "I am only a man myself."

While talking with him, Peter went inside and found a large gathering of people. He said to them: "You are well aware that it is against our law for a Jew to associate with or visit a Gentile. But God has shown me that I should not call anyone impure or unclean. So when I was sent for, I came without raising any objection…"

Then Peter began to speak: "I now realize how true it is that God does not show favoritism but accepts from every nation the one who fears him and does what is right." (Acts 10:25-29, 34-35)

I can't remember when I first realized my main spiritual gift is teaching. I only know that at the tender age of 6, before I became a Christian, I asked Mama if I could have a school in our screened porch. She consented, and the Crawley Kindergarten was established. I invited all the children in the neighborhood (probably 15), even older kids, and class began. Mama provided cherry Kool-aid and crackers for our snack, and I told stories, planned games, and pretty much just bossed everyone around. It was heavenly!

Some time after that, probably when either "Mary Poppins" or the Lesley Ann Warren "Cinderella" production came out, I decided to become an actress and singer. And when "The Sound of Music" arrived on my scene, my life plans were settled. I would live in Austria, be an actress, have 7 children, climb mountains, and sing for the rest of my days. (I really want to insert a laughing emoji right here!)

What I didn't plan on was letting God have any say so. However, as I grew as a Christian and came to realize what kind of lifestyle I might be committing to, I began asking Him to guide me to His plan. I graduated from college in Music Education, but ended up going back to get my degree in Elementary Education and earned my certification in kindergarten through 8th grade in any subject, music or otherwise. In my career I taught music, kindergarten, 3rd grade, 5th grade, and 7th grade English and world history.

My "career" as a teacher in the church began while I was still in college. I offered to teach an 8th grade girls' Sunday School class and thoroughly enjoyed it. Once David and I married and moved to Beaufort, South Carolina, he and I taught junior high students. We had so much fun sharing Jesus with those kids. David would play his guitar, and we would sing lots of good old songs like, "Amazing Grace," "I Can't Wait to See Jesus," and "King Jesus."

When we moved to Opelika, Alabama, where we've lived for forty years, I began by teaching Vacation Bible School. I did that for years. Once our girls were out of the nursery, David and I started teaching 11th grade Sunday School together. We did that for 11 or 12 years before I became Preschool Minister at our church for 7 ½ years. After that, I began teaching women and have been doing that ever since.

The point is, I'm not sure when I said, "Aha! I have the spiritual gift of teaching." I just know that God gave me a love for teaching and when I'm teaching His Word, I feel more alive than when I'm doing anything else.

So what is your main gift? Gifts are made up of two categories: speaking gifts and serving gifts. Which do you feel more comfortable doing? If you're not sure, you may want to check out "Understanding and Developing Your Spiritual Gifts" at synodresourcecenter.org or "Serving God in Ministries Based on Spiritual Gifting" at mintools.com. Or take a spiritual gifts assessment online.

Read and meditate on the following passages. Ask God to nudge your heart and show you His plan.

> Each of you should use whatever gift you have received to serve others, as faithful stewards of God's grace in its various forms. If anyone speaks, they should do so as one who speaks the very words of God. If anyone serves, they should do so with the strength God provides, so that in all things God may be praised through Jesus Christ. (1 Peter 4:10-11)

> Christ chose some of us to be apostles, prophets, missionaries, pastors, and teachers, so that his people would learn to serve and his body would grow strong. This will continue until we are united by our faith and by our understanding of the Son of God. Then we will be mature, just as Christ is, and we will be completely like him. (Ephesians 4:11-13, CEV)

God's various gifts are handed out everywhere; but they all originate in God's Spirit. God's various ministries are carried out everywhere; but they all originate in God's Spirit. God's various expressions of power are in action everywhere; but God himself is behind it all. Each person is given something to do that shows who God is: Everyone gets in on it, everyone benefits. All kinds of things are handed out by the Spirit, and to all kinds of people! The variety is wonderful:

wise counsel
clear understanding
simple trust
healing the sick
miraculous acts
proclamation
distinguishing between spirits
tongues
interpretation of tongues.

All these gifts have a common origin, but are handed out one by one by the one Spirit of God. He decides who gets what, and when.

You can easily enough see how this kind of thing works by looking no further than your own body. Your body has many parts—limbs, organs, cells—but no matter how many parts you can name, you're still one body. It's exactly the same with Christ. By means of his one Spirit, we all said good-bye to our partial and piecemeal lives. We each used to independently call our own shots, but then we entered into a large and integrated life in which *he* has the final say in everything. (This is what we proclaimed in word and action when we were baptized.) Each of us is now a part of his resurrection body, refreshed and sustained at one fountain—his Spirit—where we all come to drink. The old labels we once used to identify ourselves—labels like Jew or Greek, slave or free—are no longer useful. We need something larger, more comprehensive.

I want you to think about how all this makes you more significant, not less. A body isn't just a single part blown up into something huge. It's all the different-but-similar parts arranged and functioning together. If Foot said, "I'm not elegant like Hand, embellished with rings; I guess I don't belong to this body," would that make it so? If Ear said, "I'm not beautiful like Eye, limpid and expressive; I don't deserve a place on the head," would you want to remove it from the body? If the body was all eye, how could it hear? If all ear, how could it smell? As it is, we see that God has carefully placed each part of the body right where he wanted it.

But I also want you to think about how this keeps your significance from getting blown up into self-importance. For no matter how significant you are, it is only because of what you are a *part* of. An enormous eye or a gigantic hand wouldn't be a body, but a monster. What we have is one body with many parts, each its proper size and in its proper place. No part is important on its own. Can you imagine Eye telling Hand, "Get lost; I don't need you"? Or, Head telling Foot, "You're fired; your job has been phased out"? As a matter of fact, in practice it works the other way—the "lower" the part, the more basic, and therefore necessary. You can live without an eye, for instance, but not without a stomach. When it's a part of your own body you are concerned with, it makes *no* difference whether the part is visible or clothed, higher or lower. You give it dignity and honor just as it is, without comparisons. If anything, you have more concern for the lower parts than the higher. If you had to choose, wouldn't you prefer good digestion to full-bodied hair?

The way God designed our bodies is a model for understanding our lives together as a church: every part dependent on every other part, the parts we mention and the parts we don't, the parts we see and the parts we don't. If one part hurts, every other part is involved in the hurt, and in the healing. If one part flourishes, every other part enters into the exuberance. (1 Corinthians 12:4-26, The Message)

We have different gifts, according to the grace given to each of us. If your gift is prophesying, then prophesy in accordance with your faith; if it is serving, then serve; if it is teaching, then teach; if it is to encourage, then give encouragement; if it is giving, then give generously; if it is to lead, do it diligently; if it is to show mercy, do it cheerfully. (Romans 12:6-8)

Sounds like Paul was saying, "It takes all kinds to make a church." Mama would have agreed.

Spiritual gifts are given by the Holy Spirit to be used in the body of Christ. I hope you have discovered yours and are in the process of using them to build up the body, because as Paul pointed out, it takes all spiritual gifts to make a church.

Church, however, is not just a Sunday hour or two. More and more you hear people say, "Don't just go to church. Go *be* the church." What they're saying is, our faith has got to put on boots and step into the mire of the world. So what are you good at that can be useful to your community?

Here's a true story. Mama was a really smart, book-educated woman. Her brother, on the other hand, did poorly in school. For years, they assumed that Doug was just not very smart. But he could farm land and raise animals and be so kind and gentle. He could love the Lord and take care of his aging parents and light up the room with his smile. When he was an adult, they found out he had dyslexia, and some of their questions were answered.

Fast forward to my children. Our first daughter was interested in abc's and 123's by the time she was three years old. She wanted to know how to spell everything and labeled all her drawings with words. One Saturday morning when she was five and a half, she woke up being able to read the newspaper. It had just clicked, seemingly overnight.

Our second daughter was not interested in letters or numbers. She liked blocks and puzzles and being outside and balls and wheels, but she had no interest in academics. When she went to kindergarten, she was two months shy of being six years old, and she knew two letters of the alphabet - S and B (her name was Shelley Bazemore). I'm ashamed to admit it, but I truly thought she was dumb.

Then God did what I call a "God thing." Grace and Shelley were at school and their twin sisters were at home napping, so I was kicked back with the Reader's Digest for a few minutes. And there it was: an article entitled something like "The Theory of Multiple Intelligences." A man named Howard Gardner had proposed that there are seven different types of intelligence rather than just the do-well-in-school type. These are the categories he suggested:

1. musical-rhythmic,
2. visual-spatial,

3. verbal-linguistic,
4. logical-mathematical,
5. bodily-kinesthetic,
6. interpersonal,
7. intrapersonal.

When I read the article, I realized Shelley had several of these types of intelligence, and I began to look at her in a different way. I encouraged her to use the skills and interests she had, and of course she learned to read and write and do all that stuff really well, too.

Since 1983, Gardner has added two or three more categories to his theory. You can read more about it if you want to. My point here is that we are all given talents that God can use to bless the people he places in our lives.

> Then Moses said to the people of Israel, "See, the Lord has called by name Bezalel the son of Uri, son of Hur, of the tribe of Judah; and he has filled him with the Spirit of God, with skill, with intelligence, with knowledge, and with all craftsmanship, to devise artistic designs, to work in gold and silver and bronze, in cutting stones for setting, and in carving wood, for work in every skilled craft. And he has inspired him to teach, both him and Oholiab the son of Ahisamach of the tribe of Dan. He has filled them with skill to do every sort of work done by an engraver or by a designer or by an embroiderer in blue and purple and scarlet yarns and fine twined linen, or by a weaver—by any sort of workman or skilled designer. (Exodus 35:30-35)

> An excellent wife who can find?
> She is far more precious than jewels.

The heart of her husband trusts in her,
    and he will have no lack of gain.
She does him good, and not harm,
    all the days of her life.
She seeks wool and flax,
    and works with willing hands.
She is like the ships of the merchant;
    she brings her food from afar.
She rises while it is yet night
    and provides food for her household
    and portions for her maidens.
She considers a field and buys it;
    with the fruit of her hands she plants a vineyard.
She dresses herself with strength
    and makes her arms strong.
She perceives that her merchandise is profitable.
    Her lamp does not go out at night.
She puts her hands to the distaff,
    and her hands hold the spindle.

She opens her hand to the poor
    and reaches out her hands to the needy.
She is not afraid of snow for her household,
    for all her household are clothed in scarlet.
She makes bed coverings for herself;
    her clothing is fine linen and purple.
Her husband is known in the gates
    when he sits among the elders of the land.
She makes linen garments and sells them;
    she delivers sashes to the merchant.
Strength and dignity are her clothing,
    and she laughs at the time to come.
She opens her mouth with wisdom,
    and the teaching of kindness is on her tongue.
She looks well to the ways of her household
    and does not eat the bread of idleness.
Her children rise up and call her blessed;
    her husband also, and he praises her:

"Many women have done excellently,
  but you surpass them all."
Charm is deceitful, and beauty is vain,
  but a woman who fears the Lord is to be praised.
(Proverbs 31:10-30)

Then the King will say to those on his right, 'Come, you who are blessed by my Father, inherit the kingdom prepared for you from the foundation of the world. For I was hungry and you gave me food, I was thirsty and you gave me drink, I was a stranger and you welcomed me, I was naked and you clothed me, I was sick and you visited me, I was in prison and you came to me.' Then the righteous will answer him, saying, 'Lord, when did we see you hungry and feed you, or thirsty and give you drink? And when did we see you a stranger and welcome you, or naked and clothe you? And when did we see you sick or in prison and visit you?' And the King will answer them, 'Truly, I say to you, as you did it to one of the least of these my brothers, you did it to me.' (Matthew 25:34-40)

It takes all kinds to make a world. All kinds of intelligence and all kinds of talents and all kinds of ministries. Go do your part and make a difference.

I've said before that I'm an introvert. That doesn't mean I don't like people. I love laughter and conversation and having a good meal with friends. But when it's time to recharge my batteries, I do it best alone. You're either nodding your head or wondering *What*!?

While I always knew I didn't react to things exactly the way other people did, I wasn't aware of the four temperaments until I was an adult. A middle-aged adult. Wow. Where was I all that time? Recharging my batteries alone, I guess. Anyway, when I took a temperaments assessment it all began to make sense, and I learned that I'm a phlegmatic-melancholic-sanguine. That is, I'm mainly an introvert, but I can act in an extroverted way at times. I'm mainly a "Let it Be" and "Let It Go" kind of girl, but I've been known to get frustrated when people think the rules aren't for them, and I sure do like to have a good time.

Several years ago I heard the four temperaments boiled down to four statements:

- Choleric – "Let's do things my way."
- Sanguine – "Let's do things the fun way."
- Melancholic – "Let's do things the right way."
- Phlegmatic – "Let's do things the easy way."

I learned that the first two are extroverts, and the last two are introverts. The first and third are task-oriented, and the second and fourth are people-oriented. This helped me understand so much about myself. For instance, I wanted to shut down when professors handed out the semester syllabus and I saw how much reading was required. I don't like confrontation and have a tendency to sweep difficulties under the rug. I get overwhelmed when I have to go shopping and there are too many options. (i.e. I'd rather shop for a dress in a boutique than in a department store.) I hated practicing piano. I'm a phlegmatic. Let's do things the easy way, for Pete's sake!

I'm sure for some of you, that is way too simplified. That's okay. Maybe you'll like this breakdown better:

- Choleric – the "doer"
- Sanguine – the "talker"
- Melancholic – the "thinker"
- Phlegmatic – the "watcher"

Or perhaps this one:

- Choleric – "Let's do it now!"
- Sanguine – "Trust me. It'll work out."
- Melancholic – "How was it done in the past?"
- Phlegmatic – "Let's keep things the way they are."

Whatever the catchy way of remembering or digesting the four temperaments, the truth is that we humans are different. It takes all kinds to make a world. If all of us said, "Let's do things the easy way" or "Let's keep things the way they are," nothing would ever get done. If everyone said, "Trust me. It'll work out. Let's just have some fun," nothing would ever get done. If everyone was like a bull charging through saying, "Let's do things my way, and let's do them right now!" we'd be fighting wars nonstop, and if everyone was melancholic, we'd get mired down in looking back and in all the details of life. God knew we needed all kinds in order to accomplish His purposes and in order to enjoy one another.

God saw everything that he had made, and behold, it was very good. (Genesis 1:31)

God has made us what we are, and in our union with Christ Jesus he has created us for a life of good deeds, which he has already prepared for us to do. (Ephesians 2:10, GNT)

People will come from east and west and north and south, and will take their places at the feast in the kingdom of God. (Luke 13:29)

75

Be completely humble and gentle; be patient, bearing with one another in love. Make every effort to keep the unity of the Spirit through the bond of peace. There is one body and one Spirit, just as you were called to one hope when you were called; one Lord, one faith, one baptism; one God and Father of all, who is over all and through all and in all. (Ephesians 4:2-6)

And they sang a new song, saying,

> "Worthy are you to take the scroll and to open its seals,
> for you were slain, and by your blood you ransomed people
> for God from every tribe and language and people and
> nation..." (Rev. 5:9)

*I don't remember Mama ever making this. She probably did, and I probably whined about tasting it, but it sounds delicious to me now.

Ratatouille

1 medium eggplant (about 1 pound), cut lengthwise into quarters and sliced
3 medium zucchini, sliced
2 medium green peppers, sliced lengthwise, seeds removed
1 large onion, sliced thin
2 medium tomatoes, peeled and cut in wedges
2 cloves garlic, crushed
2 cups sliced mushrooms
vegetable oil (I use avocado oil)
salt and pepper
1 medium jar spaghetti sauce (I use Rao's)
Parmesan cheese

Pour one –quarter inch oil in large skillet and heat. Add oil as needed. Saute eggplant about 10 minutes on each side, remove with slotted spoon. Saute zucchini about 10 minutes or until tender. Layer over eggplant. Salt and pepper each vegetable layer lightly, Saute green pepper and onion about 5 minutes. Layer all in dish. Saute tomato wedges about 2 ½ minutes and remove. Saute mushrooms until golden. Place on top other vegetable layers. Pour spaghetti sauce over vegetables to barely cover. Sprinkle with Parmesan cheese. The dish may be refrigerated at this point. Before serving, place in cold oven, uncovered. Turn oven to 250 degrees and heat vegetables for 45 minutes. Serves 10.

Ratatouille Quiche

Place leftover ratatouille in uncooked pie shell. Combine 2 large eggs, 2/3 cup milk, 1/8 tsp. nutmeg, dash of salt and pepper. Pour egg mixture over vegetables in pie shell. Bake in 350 oven for 30 minutes.

"Enough is Enough!"

In almost every family, one of the parents is more of a disciplinarian than the other. In our house, it was Mama, because Daddy traveled a great deal for his job. Mama was loving and kind and smiled a lot, but when she said, "Enough is enough" with that look on her face, you knew she was SERIOUS. You had better stop what you were doing and fly right because what she meant was, "Enough shenanigans, sass, silliness, or else."

I don't know whether my husband is just too sweet to scare kids into line or whether I inherited Mama's facial muscles. I just know I've got "the look" down pat. And I've shortened Mama's phrase to "Stop." No nonsense. No explanations. Just "Stop." Doesn't always work, but sometimes it's pretty magical.

Tying this saying of Mama's to a spiritual truth is a little difficult because God is so patient. He smiles on us (Numbers 6:24-26) and sings over us (Zephaniah 3:17). He gives two, three, four, even seven times seventy chances. He forgives and rescues again and again. Nevertheless, I was able to come up with a few examples that seem to be God saying, "Enough is enough!"

#1 (This is the most important, not the first one in the Bible):

"When the fullness of time was come, God sent forth his Son,... to redeem them that were under the law..." (Galatians 4:4-5, KJV)

In other words, "When enough was enough, God sent Jesus" (my paraphrase).

It would be impossible for me to go back to the beginning of the Bible and explain all God's thoughts and plans, particularly because I don't presume to understand the tiniest percentage of God's thoughts. However, scripture makes it clear that God established a covenant (sacred agreement) with Abraham that said, "Trust and obey me, and I will be with you and bless you." And Abraham trusted God. His faith was counted as righteousness even though he was a human with human failings like you and me.

Four hundred and thirty years later, God gave His people the Law, not because faith wasn't enough anymore but because they needed to see how sinful they were. God wanted them to see how much they needed Him. His covenant was the same: "Trust me, obey me, and I will be with you and bless you." But instead of the people saying, "We are so sinful, Lord God, and we need you every moment every day," they made a god of the Law. They added to the Law. They became prideful through obedience to the Law. They left God out and trusted their own behavior.

God persevered. He chose judges, prophets, priests, and kings through whom He tried to bring the people back to faith in Him and fellowship with Him. And for a while, the people would turn back to God. Then off they'd go again. Back to rebellion. Back to the law. Back to pride. (Reminds me of my yo-yo dieting, and it was just as successful.)

Then God said, "Enough is enough! No more yo-yo trusting. No more yo-yo obedience. No more yo-yo righteousness. The Law cannot save you!" (This might not be an actual quote from God, but you get the drift.)

Think on Galatians 3:21 – 4:7, TLB, below (my emphasis).

If we could be saved by his laws, then God would not have had to give us a different way to get out of the grip of sin—for the Scriptures insist we are all its prisoners. The only way out is through faith in Jesus Christ; the way of escape is open to all who believe him.

Until Christ came we were guarded by the law, kept in protective custody, so to speak, until we could believe in the coming Savior.

Let me put it another way. The Jewish laws were our teacher and guide until Christ came to give us right standing with God through our faith. But now that Christ has come, we don't need those laws any longer to guard us and lead us to him. For now we are all children of God through faith in Jesus Christ, and we who have been baptized into union with Christ are enveloped by him. We are no longer Jews or Greeks or slaves or free men or even merely men or women, but we are all the same—we are Christians; we are one in Christ Jesus. And now that we are Christ's we are the true descendants of Abraham, and all of God's promises to him belong to us...

We were slaves to Jewish laws and rituals, for we thought they could save us. **But when the right time came, the time God decided on, he sent his Son, born of a woman, born as a Jew, to buy freedom for us who were slaves to the law so that he could adopt us as his very own sons.** And because we are his sons, God has sent the Spirit of his Son into our hearts, so now we can rightly speak of God as our dear Father. Now we are no longer slaves but God's own sons. And since we are his sons, everything he has belongs to us, for that is the way God planned.

Are you trusting in yourself (your own good and kind thoughts, your own behavior, your own abilities, your own bank account, your own ideas and opinions) to get you to heaven? Stop. There is only one Savior, and that is Jesus Christ. I want to invite you to put your trust in Him right now. He died a horrible death on the cross to take all your sin upon Himself. He bought your freedom. Admit that you are a sinner and need a Savior. Ask Him to be your Savior. God wants to be your very own dear Father. Accept His gift of Jesus and live in sonship and freedom from this day on.

Has there ever been a child who would take "No" for an answer? Somehow children think if they ask again one hundred times, the answer will change. And maybe for some parents it does because, as a rule, parents give out of energy before children do. If I had a nickel for every time I repeated, "I said 'No'" or "Don't ask me again," I'd have a lot of nickels.

Has God ever told you "No"? I'll answer for you. Yes, He has. He has told us all "No" many times in His word. A few examples are:

"Let me love myself, my family, and my friends more than I love you." "No."

"Let me worship idols." "No."

"Let me use your name as an expletive." "No."

"Let me work or entertain myself instead of resting and worshiping You." "No."

"Let me disrespect my parents." "No."

"Let me murder him." "No."

"Let me have an affair." "No."

"Let me take something without paying for it." "No."

"Let me lie about her." "No."

"Let me compare myself to everyone else and want to have what everyone else has." "No."

Did you recognize those as the Ten Commandments? As I mentioned yesterday, God gave these "shalt nots" to show His people just how sinful they were and how much they needed Him. But God said "No" to these desires for a couple of other reasons, too. First, He knows what will hurt us now or be bad for us in the long run. So when He says "No" to something, it's for our good. Another reason is that He will not allow anyone to steal His glory. Like with Moses:

> Now there was no water for the community, and the people gathered in opposition to Moses and Aaron. They quarreled with Moses and said, "If only we had died when our brothers fell dead before the Lord! Why did you bring the Lord's community into this wilderness, that we and our livestock should die here? Why did you bring us up out of Egypt to this terrible place? It has no grain or figs, grapevines or pomegranates. And there is no water to drink!"

> Moses and Aaron went from the assembly to the entrance to the tent of meeting and fell facedown, and the glory of the Lord appeared to them. The Lord said to Moses, "Take the staff, and you and your brother Aaron gather the assembly together. Speak

to that rock before their eyes and it will pour out its water. You will bring water out of the rock for the community so they and their livestock can drink."

So Moses took the staff from the Lord's presence, just as he commanded him. He and Aaron gathered the assembly together in front of the rock and Moses said to them, "Listen, you rebels, must we bring you water out of this rock?" Then Moses raised his arm and struck the rock twice with his staff. Water gushed out, and the community and their livestock drank.

But the Lord said to Moses and Aaron, "Because you did not trust in me enough to honor me as holy in the sight of the Israelites [because you stole my glory], you will not bring this community into the land I give them." (Numbers 20:2-12)

So Moses and Aaron weren't allowed to enter the Promised Land. Later, right before the Israelites crossed the Jordan to enter that land, Moses described all that had happened since they had left Egypt. Listen to Moses reporting this bit:

At that time I pleaded with the Lord: "Sovereign Lord, you have begun to show your servant your greatness and your strong hand. For what god is there in heaven

or on earth who can do the deeds and mighty works you do? Let me go over and see the good land beyond the Jordan—that fine hill country and Lebanon."

But because of you [the Israelites] the Lord was angry with me and would not listen to me. "That is **enough**," the Lord said. "Do not speak to me anymore about this matter. Go up to the top of Pisgah and look west and north and south and east. Look at the land with your own eyes, since you are not going to cross this Jordan..." (Deut 3:23-27, my emphasis)

Just like a child, Moses blamed other people for his own bad behavior, and just like a child, Moses pestered God to change His mind about letting him go into the Promised Land. But God said, "Enough is enough. Hush."

Listen, if God has already plainly said "No," we don't need to ask again. When He says, "Enough!" we just need to trust that He is protecting the display of His glory or protecting us from harm.

Thank Him right now for loving you enough to say "No."

❧

Have you seen the "You Had One Job" meme? It's images of ridiculous mistakes people have made in carrying out a seemingly simple job. Such as a grocery store display of fruit juices under a sign that proclaims "Juicy Bacon" (funny, but not a big deal) or hamburger buns in a hotdog bun wrapper (not too big a deal, maybe) or a road sign that shows a curve to the right when the curve in the road goes left (pretty big deal).

When Jesus went to the Garden of Gethsemane, he gave Peter, James, and John, the inner circle of His disciples, one job to do.

> They went to a place called Gethsemane, and Jesus said to his disciples, "Sit here while I pray." He took Peter, James and John along with him, and he began to be deeply distressed and troubled. "My soul is overwhelmed with sorrow to the point of death," he said to them. "Stay here and keep watch."
>
> Going a little farther, he fell to the ground and prayed that if

85

possible the hour might pass from him. *"Abba*, Father," he said, "everything is possible for you. Take this cup from me. Yet not what I will, but what you will."

Then he returned to his disciples and found them sleeping. "Simon," he said to Peter, "are you asleep? Couldn't you keep watch for one hour? Watch and pray so that you will not fall into temptation. The spirit is willing, but the flesh is weak."

Once more he went away and prayed the same thing. When he came back, he again found them sleeping, because their eyes were heavy. They did not know what to say to him.

Returning the third time, he said to them, "Are you still sleeping and resting? **Enough!** The hour has come. Look, the Son of Man is delivered into the hands of sinners.   (Mark 14:32-41 my emphasis)

Can you feel Jesus' frustration? Can you see the sheepish looks the three probably gave Him? Do you know that when Jesus ascended into heaven a little over a month after His resurrection, He left these men and His other followers just one job to do?

"Go and make disciples of all nations, baptizing them in the name of the Father and of the Son and of the Holy Spirit, and teaching them to obey everything I have commanded you." (Matthew 28:19-20).

"You will receive power when the Holy Spirit comes on you; and you will be my witnesses in Jerusalem, and in all Judea and Samaria, and to the ends of the earth."(Acts 1:8)

Just in case we need a refresher course, here is the gospel in a nutshell (Colossians 1:19-22):

> For God was pleased to have all his fullness dwell in [Jesus], and through [Jesus] to reconcile to himself all things, whether things on earth or things in heaven, by making peace through [Jesus'] blood, shed on the cross.
>
> Once you were alienated from God and were enemies in your minds because of your evil behavior. But now he has reconciled you by Christ's physical body through death to present you holy in his sight, without blemish and free from accusation.

It's pretty easy for me to read the account of the disciples falling asleep and think, *Aw, what's the big deal? After all, they were human. They were stressed out. And don't forget, even God rested! Is resting/sleeping such a bad thing?* Jesus knew what His disciples were about to face. He knew they would need spiritual strength to combat the persecution and fear. He knew they hadn't really understood that He was about to die. He knew it was a huge deal. So He said "Enough!"

Let's translate this to our culture. Is seeking an escape through entertainment or sports or vacation or sleep such a bad thing? After all, we're human. What's the big deal? The big deal is this, folks. Jesus gave us one job to do, and instead we're mostly doing everything else. We're working. We're playing. We're spending tons of time on social media. We're using up our energy on pursuing meaningless pastimes or inconsequential knowledge or material possessions.

I fiercely believe that Jesus is saying, "Enough! The hour has come." He knows we need spiritual strength to face the persecution and fear that is coming. Also, He is well aware that many in our world are going to hell. He yearns for us to pray and then get up and give of ourselves and love others and proclaim the gospel.

I had an argument with my husband. Alas, I am not perfect. We fought over how to get home from the beach. He thought he knew how, but we had gone to a different beach than we sometimes do, so we needed to go home a different way. I was adamant about that. And I was determined to use my smart phone because, though I knew the way he wanted to go was waaaay out of the way, I had no idea how to get home from where we were.

Guess what I found out after we had exchanged heated words for a few minutes? Though we were both angry, neither one of us was particularly angry about the route we were driving. David was upset that we didn't stay in a caravan with our daughter's car (he wanted us all to stay together as a happy family). I was mad because he didn't trust me to get us home (he has early onset Alzheimer's, and I have had to take on the task of navigation on vacations).

This sort of thing happens often with people, I've found. We think we're upset about one thing and it's really something else. Or we get mad at one person when another person or situation should have our attention. Or we're exhausted. Or hungry. Or slightly insane.

Jesus said, "Enough" to this. Listen to Luke 22:36-38, 47-51:

> He said to them, "But now if you have a purse, take it, and also a bag; and if you don't have a sword, sell your cloak and buy one…"

> The disciples said, "See, Lord, here are two swords."

"That is enough," he replied....

While he was still speaking a crowd came up, and the man who was called Judas, one of the Twelve, was leading them. He approached Jesus to kiss him, but Jesus asked him, "Judas, are you betraying the Son of Man with a kiss?"

When Jesus' followers saw what was going to happen, they said, "Lord, should we strike with our swords?" And one of them struck the servant of the high priest, cutting off his right ear.

But Jesus answered, "**No more of this!**" And he touched the man's ear and healed him. (Luke 22:36-38 and 47-51, my emphasis)

Jesus knew His disciples would face persecution and that since He would not be around, they might have to protect themselves. Thus, the need for swords. So why did he get upset when one of them used his sword against the servant of the high priest?

> Premature action.
> Wrong enemy.
> Bad witness.

Are you upset at anybody or about anything? Are you sure you're fighting the right enemy? Have you asked Jesus whether to "strike with your sword"? Have you listened for His reply? Do you know that your response in this matter will be a witness?

Two things for us to contemplate today:

1. Haven't we done enough already of focusing our anger on the wrong subject? Ephesians 6:11-13 reminds us:

Put on the full armor of God, so that you can take your stand against the devil's schemes. For our struggle is not against flesh and blood, but against the rulers, against the authorities, against the powers of this dark world and against the spiritual forces of evil in the heavenly realms. Therefore put on the full armor of God, so that when the day of evil comes, you may be able to stand your ground, and after you have done everything, to stand.

2. Jesus *is* enough. He can heal the wounds we've created or experienced if we ask Him.

Let's look at this truth: "Jesus *is* enough."

And with all his abundant wealth through Christ Jesus, my God will supply **all your needs.** (Philippians 4:19, GNT, my emphasis)

And God is able to bless you abundantly, so that in all things at all times, **having all that you need**, you will abound in every good work. (2 Corinthians 9:8, my emphasis)

We have **everything we need** to live a life that pleases God. It was all given to us by God's own power, when we learned that he had invited us to share in his wonderful goodness. (2 Peter 1:3, CEV, my emphasis)

Praise be to the God and Father of our Lord Jesus Christ, who has blessed us in the heavenly realms with **every spiritual blessing in Christ.** (Ephesians 1:3, my emphasis)

In the next eleven verses, Paul goes on to describe these blessings.

They are:

1. I am chosen (predestined).
2. I am holy and without fault.
3. I am adopted.
4. I've received grace.
5. I am redeemed (set free by the paying of a ransom).
6. I've been forgiven.
7. I can know the mystery of His will (the church).
8. I have hope.
9. I am included (part of the body).
10. I am sealed with the Holy Spirit, who guarantees my inheritance.

Interspersed among the list of blessings are these sweet phrases that remind us how good God's plan for us is:

> in his sight
> in love
> in accordance with his pleasure
> lavished on us
> with all wisdom and understanding
> according to his good pleasure
> according to the plan of him who works out everything in conformity with the purpose of
> his will
> for the praise of his glory

Which blessing is the most precious to you? Why?

Which "feel good" phrase above speaks to your heart the most?

Is Jesus enough for you?

Take a moment to thank God for his glorious riches in Christ Jesus.

*Today's recipe is from me, and I got it from Jane Carter. I don't know where Jane got it.

Every delightful, scrumptious blessing is in this cornbread. It probably has a kazillion calories per serving, but I haven't found anyone who cares!

Corn and Cheese Squares

2 (8 ½ ounce) packages cornbread mix

1 tsp. salt

1 cup chopped green onion (scallions)

1 tsp. parsley

3 Tbsp. chopped fresh or pickled jalapeno peppers

1 cup sour cream

1 cup small curd cottage cheese

¾ cup butter, melted (I use ½ cup)

4 eggs

1 (16 ounce) package frozen corn with red and green peppers, thawed and drained (I use two cans Mexicorn, drained)

4 ounces sharp cheddar, grated

In a large bowl combine all ingredients and mix well. Spread batter in greased 9 x 13 pan. Bake in pre-heated 400 degree oven for 35-40 minutes or until brown. Let cool 10 min. Cut and serve hot.

"Everything's Better with Butter or Cream"

L ong before the Food Network became a cultural marvel, Mama knew what made good food. She'd exclaim, "Everything's better with butter or cream," and I would have to agree. Fish tastes better when cooked in butter. A wholesome baked sweet potato? Heavenly with butter. Broccoli is my favorite green vegetable and delicious when quick-sautéed in butter, of course. Or spinach, the super food of one well-known "musckle"-bound sailor. If you have your choice, take it sautéed in butter. Mmm. Or creamed spinach is also delightful. Creamed corn, creamed potatoes, strawberries and cream, cream of tomato soup, cream in my coffee, whipped cream. Yum! Everything's better with butter or cream.

Here is an exciting spiritual parallel: Everything's better with praise and worship. How bleak our lives seem at times. Listen to the psalmist:

> I am in distress;
> my eyes grow weak with sorrow,
> my soul and body with grief.
> My life is consumed by anguish
> and my years by groaning;
> my strength fails because of my affliction,
> and my bones grow weak.

> Because of all my enemies,
> I am the utter contempt of my neighbors
> and an object of dread to my closest friends—
> those who see me on the street flee from me.
> I am forgotten as though I were dead;
> I have become like broken pottery. (Psalm 31:9-12)

His life seems hard to swallow, sort of like the bitterness of Brussels sprouts. But when he adds praise and worship, watch his outlook change:

> But I trust in you, LORD;
> I say, "You are my God."
> How abundant are the good things
>   that you have stored up for those who fear you,
> Praise be to the LORD,
> for he showed me the wonders of his love
> when I was in a city under siege.
> In my alarm I said,
> I am cut off from your sight!"
> Yet you heard my cry for mercy
> when I called to you for help. (Psalm 31:14, 19, 21-22)

We find this pattern repeated in the psalms:

"Poor, pitiful me" + Praise = New Perspective

How about you? Can you recall a moment or period when you felt defeated, scared or angry? Was your life unpalatable? Are you going through such a season right now? Do you believe everything's better with praise and worship? Paul and Silas must have. When they were beaten, thrown in prison and shackled in chains, when night came and they felt lonely and afraid, they chose to sing songs of praise to God (Acts 16:25). Have you learned that praising God in the midst of painful or hard to swallow circumstances is like pouring sweet, melted butter on those distasteful Brussels sprouts? And what about the role of praise and worship on a great day? It makes the day even better, like dipping sweet strawberries in luscious whipped cream. Whatever your feelings or circumstances, try praising God right now. Start with several verses from Psalm 96:2, 6-7:

> Come to worship him with thankful hearts
> and songs of praise.
> Bow down and worship
> the Lord our Creator!
> The Lord is our God, and we are his people,
> the sheep he takes care of in his own pasture.

When I was a girl, we had a neighbor boy whose nickname was Nunu. He was an odd sort of fellow, and so the nickname fit. But what Nunu is most remembered for - by me, anyway – is walking around his front yard eating a stick of butter. Yes, you heard correctly. Now, I like butter; it's delicious. But you will never see me eating a stick like it's an ice cream cone or lollipop. That's butter overload, a little strange and quite repulsive.

That's how some people feel about praising the Lord. A little bit is nice, even preferable. But don't go overboard. Don't be walking around the front yard letting everyone see and hear you praising at the top of your lungs, or worse yet, raising your arms while you praise. That's just a little strange and quite repulsive. We've got dignity to preserve here in this neighborhood and in our church!

Reminds me of 2 Samuel 6:12-16, 20-22:

> Now King David was told, "The Lord has blessed the household of Obed-Edom and everything he has, because of the ark of God." So David went to bring up the ark of God from the house of Obed-Edom to the City of David with rejoicing.

> When those who were carrying the ark of the Lord had taken six steps, he sacrificed a bull and a fattened calf. Wearing a linen ephod, David was dancing before the Lord with all his might, while he and all Israel were bringing up the ark of the Lord with shouts and the sound of trumpets.

> As the ark of the Lord was entering the City of David, Michal [wife of King David] daughter of Saul watched from a window. And when she saw King David leaping and dancing before the Lord, she despised him in her heart...

> When David returned home to bless his household, Michal daughter of Saul came out to meet him and said, "How the king of Israel has distinguished himself today, going around half-naked in full view of the slave girls of his servants as any vulgar fellow would!"

> David said to Michal, "It was before the Lord, who chose me rather than your father or anyone from his house when he appointed me ruler over the Lord's people Israel—I will celebrate before the Lord. I will become even more undignified than this, and I will be humiliated in my own eyes.

Who was David dancing for? Why?

David says that he would become even more "undignified" and

"humiliated." What did he mean?

So here are some wrong questions concerning praise:

- Who is watching?
- How much is enough?
- What will it get me?

And here are some of the right questions.

- Who do we worship?
- Why do we praise?
- How much is too much?

Praise God using Psalm 96:1-6 (below).

Sing a new song to the Lord!
Let the whole earth sing to the Lord!
[2] Sing to the Lord; praise his name.
Each day proclaim the good news that he saves.
[3] Publish his glorious deeds among the nations.
Tell everyone about the amazing things he does.
[4] Great is the Lord! He is most worthy of praise!
He is to be feared above all gods.
[5] The gods of other nations are mere idols,
but the Lord made the heavens!
[6] Honor and majesty surround him;
strength and beauty fill his sanctuary.

Sweets are my downfall. I try to choose "good" sweets like fruit and dark chocolate. Well, that's a lie. Sometimes I choose good sweets.

But sometimes I just want black bottom pie.

Pie crust. Yum.

Dark chocolate custard. Yummy.

Custard chiffon. Mmmm.

Whipped heavy cream. Aaahhh! (Can you hear me singing?)

I'm somewhat ashamed to say that I get really excited about eating a piece of black bottom pie (a large piece). Did I tell you it's pretty to look at, too? First comes the looking, then the dipping of the fork. Then the closing of the eyes as the pie goes in the mouth. It is one of the good gifts from God. So it's okay to eat it. It's a spiritual thing.

Worship has layers. Each as good as the others. Psalm 100 (KJV) has always been a favorite of mine. I memorized it early on, and the layers of worship depicted continually thrill me:

Make a joyful noise unto the Lord, all ye lands.

Serve the Lord with gladness: come before his presence with singing.

Know ye that the Lord he is God: it is he that hath made us, and not we ourselves; we are his people, and the sheep of his pasture.

Enter into his gates with thanksgiving, and into his courts with praise: be thankful unto him, and bless his name.

For the Lord is good; his mercy is everlasting; and his truth endureth to all generations.

The Lord is good; his mercy lasts forever, and he will always be truthful, righteous, and just. He made us, so He knows us. He knows how we think. He knows what we need. He knows how to best love us. He knows. So,

Everybody everywhere, give the Lord a shout out!

Sing to Him.
Thank Him.
Praise Him.
Bless Him.
Serve Him.
With gladness!
Know Him.
Aaahhh.

ॐ

My husband supposedly hates butter, sour cream, cream cheese, and cream sauces/soups. But he loves potato casserole (butter, sour cream *and* cream of chicken soup), chess squares (butter and cream cheese), yogurt (which is basically sour milk or cream), strawberry cake (cream cheese and butter frosting), et cetera. I think you get the picture.

It's kind of like the butter thing all over again. Most of us are not going to eat butter straight. Or sour cream or cream cheese or cream sauce. But as ingredients on top of something or in something else, they are fabulous, maybe even stupendous. I mean, cream cheese pound cake is so much better than ordinary pound cake. It just is.

Sometimes our praise and worship becomes rote. I have friends who are Methodists, and they say that sometimes their liturgical rituals (songs, prayers, etc.) can become automatic and boring. But you

99

know what? Other church's praise and worship can be lifeless as well. Why? Because we're just saying the words. Repeating something we've memorized. Watching and judging the people around us. Wondering why the worship leader chose this song again. Hoping the late-arriving visitor is not thinking of crowding onto "our" pew/row.

It's like we're eating cream cheese straight from the shiny silver package, and it's not necessarily distasteful, but it sure is blah. What other ingredients can we add that will make it exciting, meaningful, and not at all distasteful to us or to God?

Maybe purity of heart? ("Blessed are the pure in heart, for they shall see God." Matthew 5:8) That means my motive for worship has to be pure. I may need to ask myself why I'm there. Is it for God, or is it to check it off my 'To Do' list? Am I there to be seen, or am I there to see God?

Maybe I need to be sure the object of my worship is really Jesus. ("Do not worship any god except me. Do not make idols that look like anything in the sky or on earth or in the ocean under the earth. Don't bow down and worship idols. I am the Lord your God, and I demand all your love." Exodus 20:3-5, CEV) He is the only One who merits my devotion. He is the worthy Lamb who was slain and our worship should be nothing else and nothing less than giving Him the power, riches, wisdom, strength, honor, glory, and blessing he deserves (Revelation 5:12).

Perhaps I'm pure in my motives and in the One I worship, but I just can't seem to put away distraction. Maybe it's because I go to worship without clothing myself in prayer. ("About midnight Paul and Silas were praying and singing praises to God, while the other prisoners listened. Suddenly a strong earthquake shook the jail to its foundations. The doors opened, and the chains fell from all the prisoners." Acts 16:25-26, CEV) If I want astonishing things to happen when I worship, I'm going to need to pray more and to be in expectation more.

After all that, if I'm still eating cream cheese instead of cream cheese pound cake, could it be that I'm just not allowing the Holy Spirit to participate in my worship? Am I afraid of what others will think? Am I afraid of what God may ask me to do? Do I have God in a small box of my making instead of opening my small heart to the immensity of the everlasting Almighty God of the universe? ("God is spirit, and his worshipers must worship in the Spirit and in truth." John 4:24)

It's true that from time to time praise and worship can be beautifully spontaneous, but most of the time, we need to take time to prepare our hearts, and when we do, the worship experience is so much better. It just is.

Today we are going to worship using Psalm 103. In verses 3 through 7, I have emphasized the Lord's "benefits" (blessings). As you read, insert your name in the blanks and meditate on what that means in your life.

> ^{1} Praise the Lord, my soul;
> all my inmost being, praise his holy name.
> ^{2} Praise the Lord, my soul,
> and forget not all his benefits—
> ^{3} who **forgives** all _____'s sins

and **heals** all _____'s diseases,

4 who **redeems** _____'s life from the pit

and **crowns** _____ with love and compassion,

⁵ who **satisfies** _____'s desires with good things

so that your youth is renewed like the eagle's.

⁶ The Lord **works righteousness** **and justice for** all the oppressed.

⁷ He **made known his ways to** Moses,

his deeds to the people of Israel:

⁸ The Lord is compassionate and gracious,

slow to anger, abounding in love.

⁹ He will not always accuse,

 nor will he harbor his anger forever;

¹⁰ he does not treat us as our sins deserve

 or repay us according to our iniquities.

¹¹ For as high as the heavens are above the earth,

so great is his love for those who fear him;

¹² as far as the east is from the west,

 so far has he removed our transgressions from us.

¹³ As a father has compassion on his children,

 so the Lord has compassion on those who fear him;

Verses 8 through 13 elaborate on the topic of God's forgiveness. First, in verse 8, the psalmist describes the attributes of God that make Him a forgiving God. What are the attributes?

Which of those attributes is described further in verse 9? Which in verse 10? Verse 11? Verse 12?

Verse 13 is a recap of the previous truths. We who are parents understand having compassion on our children. They can be naughty, haughty, irresponsible, or irrepressible, yet we love them, we try to find ways to help them, and we forgive them. We know they are the product of two people who aren't perfect.

Here's an amazing truth about God's compassion and forgiveness: He remembers we are dust - here today, gone tomorrow:

[14] for he knows how we are formed,
he remembers that we are dust.
[15] The life of mortals is like grass,
   they flourish like a flower of the field;
[16] the wind blows over it and it is gone,
   and its place remembers it no more.
[17] But from everlasting to everlasting
   the Lord's love is with those who fear him,
and his righteousness with their children's children—
[18] with those who keep his covenant
   and remember to obey his precepts.
[19] The Lord has established his throne in heaven,
and his kingdom rules over all.
[20] Praise the Lord, you his angels,
   you mighty ones who do his bidding,
   who obey his word.
[21] Praise the Lord, all his heavenly hosts,
you his servants who do his will.
[22] Praise the Lord, all his works
   everywhere in his dominion.
Praise the Lord, my soul.

Verse 17 begins with the word *But*. In this case, it means *"In spite of what I just said..."* In spite of the fact that I am dust, a blade of grass that grows and then is blown away in an instant, the Lord is still the everlasting God who loves me. Me! And He promises to be good to my grandchildren just because I revere Him. Now that is what I call gracious. Thank you, Lord!

If you're like me (and have grandchildren), you are a bit concerned about their futures in this world and this country. But verse 19 is a reminder that "Greater is He that is in me than He that is in the world." He rules. He reigns. He is love from generation to generation. Let's praise Him!

Go back now and reread the whole Psalm aloud, worshipping God as you read. If you feel compelled, shout out, sing, dance before the Lord. He is GOOD.

*Mama noted that today's recipe was from Better Homes and Gardens magazine. The original recipe was for one pie, but I've tweaked it and always make two. You can make one, but you're going to want 2.

Black Bottom Pie

(Makes 2)

2 deep dish piecrusts, baked according to directions (Do this first!)
1 ½ cups sugar, divided
1 ½ Tablespoons cornstarch
3 cups milk, scalded
6 eggs, separated
1 ½ cups semi-sweet chocolate chips
1 ½ Tablespoons unflavored gelatin (this is about 2 packets)
¾ cup cold water
2 cups heavy cream, whipped with 6 Tablespoons sugar

- Bake piecrusts. Let cool.

- Separate eggs. Beat the egg yolks.

- Scald milk (bring to a boil while stirring, then take off heat) in heavy saucepan.

- Combine ¾ cup sugar and cornstarch in top of double boiler. Set aside.

- Slowly add scalded milk to egg yolks, stirring constantly. Stir this mixture into the sugar/cornstarch mixture.

- Cook in the top of double boiler until the custard coats a spoon.

- To two cups of the custard, add chocolate chips and stir until melted. Pour evenly in the bottom of the two cooled piecrusts. Refrigerate.

- Soften the gelatin in the cold water. Add to remaining custard. Stir until gelatin is dissolved. Chill until slightly thick (30-40 minutes. I check it after 20, 25, 30, 35 to make sure it doesn't gel. It should just be cooled and slightly thickened.)

- Beat egg whites, adding ¾ cup sugar gradually, until mixture stands in soft peaks. Fold in the custard/gelatin mixture. Pour evenly over chocolate layer in the pies (You will have too much of the meringue mixture. Throw the excess away ☹). Refrigerate.

- Beat heavy cream, adding 6 T. sugar gradually, until peaks form. Spoon onto pies. Chill thoroughly.

Keep pie refrigerated - if there are any leftovers, that is!

"The Only Thing Wrong with People's Sunday Mornings Is Their Saturday Nights"

Mama's breakfast calendar was organized and simple. On Mondays, Wednesdays, and Fridays, we had bacon, eggs, and toast with our orange juice and milk. Tuesday and Thursday were pancake and waffle with sausage days, respectively. Cereal was for Saturday, and Sunday, well, Sunday was church day. Mama was the Minister of Music at our church, so Sunday was busy from early morning till bedtime. So on Saturday, Mama went to Krispy Kreme, and Sunday morning we ate a quick donut and went to church.

That's how I grew up. You didn't have to decide what to eat for breakfast and you didn't have to decide if you were going to church this week. You didn't base your church attendance on what else might be on the calendar. Instead, you planned the rest of your schedule around worship on Sunday. That was life in the Crawley household. Actually, that was life in a great percentage of households of the 50's and 60's when I was growing up.

But sometimes people didn't make it to church, and that's when Mama would say, "The only thing wrong with their Sunday morning is their Saturday night." Maybe they stayed out too late, and the children were exhausted. Or perhaps they had a few too many drinks and were hung over on Sunday morning. During the summer months, the problem was usually that people ended up staying at the river instead of coming back to the city on Saturday night. Whatever the reason, Mama realized an essential truth: Satan doesn't want us to worship, and he will build whatever roadblock he can to detour us from worshipping God.

It used to be Saturday nights. The choices people made for Saturday nights affected their desire to get up and worship on Sundays. Now the problem has become much bigger. Our culture has become obsessed with getting ahead. Consequently, more and more women have entered the workplace. In addition, parents have enrolled their children in a myriad of extracurricular academic, musical, and athletic pursuits that fill practically every waking hour. As a result, real leisure time has become scarcer, and Sundays have often been dubbed "family time." If we do make it to church, frequently it is with the same "what's in it for me?" attitude that saturates our lives.

Nowadays, the only thing wrong with our Sunday mornings is really what's been wrong the whole time. We need Jesus. We need changed hearts. Then our priorities will be different. Then our primary ambition will be to worship God, our creator, redeemer, and sustainer. Psalm 145:1- 13 (CEV) shows us how:

I will praise you, my God and King, and always honor your name.
I will praise you each day and always honor your name.
You are wonderful, Lord, and you deserve all praise,
because you are much greater than anyone can understand.
Each generation will announce to the next your wonderful and powerful deeds.
I will keep thinking about your marvelous glory and your mighty miracles.

Everyone will talk about your fearsome deeds, and I will tell all nations how great you are.

They will celebrate and sing about your matchless mercy and your power to save.

You are merciful, Lord!

You are kind and patient and always loving.

You are good to everyone, and you take care of all your creation.

All creation will thank you, and your loyal people will praise you.

They will tell about your marvelous kingdom and your power.

Then everyone will know about the mighty things you do and your glorious kingdom.

Your kingdom will never end, and you will rule forever

Yesterday I was fine. *Fine* being a colorless word to describe a feeling of *Yeah, I've got problems, but who doesn't? God put me in a good place and has been very good to me. I feel somewhat fulfilled in the ministries He's given me. I have joy that can't be taken away because God loves me. Fine.*

Today I've been a basket case. Crying all day about I don't know what. Crucifying myself for all the sins in my life Jesus already died for. Feeling depressed and on a slippery slope to really depressed. And so I went for a walk. As I was trudging up hill and down in the heat, I thought, "What do psychologists say helps with depression?"

- Exercise. Check.

- Doing something for someone else. Hmm. Need to call that friend when I get back home.

- Looking for the root of the problem. Sin? Forgiven.

109

Forgotten by God.

- Diet? Maybe I need some protein or less sugar.

- Lack of nurturing relationships? Maybe. Maybe Saturday nights are not the only thing wrong with people's Sunday mornings. Maybe putting on a good face in the name of Christianity is wrong, too. Perhaps we (I) need to let people see that sometimes I'm fragile. Sometimes I sin. Sometimes I just need a friend.

I still believe that worship is for God. No doubt. But it's also for us. When my daughter and her husband lived in Lafayette, Colorado, they attended Flatirons Church. One reason they chose that fellowship was the church's motto: "Me, too." You're fragile? Me, too. You struggle with sin? Me, too. You need a friend? Me, too. You desperately need Jesus? Me, too. You want to learn how to worship Him better? Me, too.

When Jesus said His famous words, "Come unto Me, all that are weary and heavy-laden, and I will give you rest," He didn't point to one or two in the crowd and say, "You look weary. Come to Me." He said, "All you people who are weary, come to Me. All you people who are pressed down under the pressure of 'looking the part,' come to Me." Today I feel especially weary. I need Jesus, and I need a friend to come along side of me. Think I'll call Sherrie and see if she needs one, too.

I've never been as organized as Mama was. Lists, calendars, daily planner/appointment books, budget notebooks, and other such paraphernalia were trademarks of hers. Of course, writing things down used to be more necessary than it is now. Now we can set alerts on our phones to remind us to do almost anything. We are able to check our bank accounts and credit card balances from anywhere anytime. We can keep files of our files rather than lists of our lists.

But Mama had mental lists as well. Habits that helped her accomplish so much. Like going to Krispy Kreme on Saturdays. Washing on Mondays. Having her hair done on Fridays. Polishing Sunday shoes on Saturday nights. In fact, getting all of our Sunday clothes ready on Saturday nights. Making sure we weren't going to be hurried or harried before leaving for church.

When my children were small, I tried to be that organized. I would think ahead (sometimes) and get Sunday clothes ready on Saturday night. But it never failed that while I was finishing up getting myself ready for church, my husband would play with the girls, maybe even let them go outside and ride their bikes. You see where this is going, don't you? By the time I was ready, they were un-ready. Their hair would be flying out of bows and sticking to their necks and foreheads. Their slips would be hanging down below their dresses. Their shoes would be scuffed. The overall impression would be of sweaty messiness. And believe me, my Saturday night had nothing to do with my Sunday morning attitude at that point.

Can anyone identify? Has anyone else arrived at church in no mood to smile, much less worship God? Because all your plans - to be organized, on top of things, in control of your family members - have turned to dust and sweat? Because your dream of being Wonder Woman disguised in a choir robe has become just a hope that no one will notice the frown lines in your forehead and your gritted teeth?

Why do we do what we do? When we know, truly know, that beauty comes from within. That Jesus said "Come to me" not to a dressed up, organized, faultless congregation of men and women but to weary, heavy-laden unbelievers. In fact, if we look at Matthew 11:28-30 in context, we see that Jesus was rather frustrated with the group mentality. Israel as a group had rejected Him because they had been concerned with expectations and outward appearances. Vernon McGee commented, "The Lord now turns His back upon the nation Israel, no longer presenting to them the kingdom. He is on His way to the cross, and His invitation is to the individual."

McGee continues, " 'I will give you rest' is literally, 'I will rest you.' When He speaks of being 'heavy laden,' He is referring to being burdened with sin." It's hard for me to admit that wanting to be in control and wanting my family to look 'together' or 'righteous' is sin. It's easier to admit that those desires do heavy lade me. Even though my children are grown, I still care what others think of them (and me, who raised them). And somehow that pride sometimes affects my Sunday morning and makes it about me all over again. Not the good thing of being transparent as I step alongside other worshipers, but a bad thing of comparison and competition with other worshipers.

Jesus is still offering to 'rest' me. His yoke is easy and His burden is light. Let me quote McGee once more: "There is a rest which the believer experiences, and it comes through commitment and consecration to Christ. You don't have to worry about being recognized; you don't have to jockey for position if you are committed to Christ…He will put you exactly where *He* wants you when you are yoked up to Him."

That's what I need – *that* kind of rest and yoke. Krispy Kreme donuts are delicious, but I think I'll have a heaping helping of *that* before I go to church this Sunday.

Mama kept her daily list, prayer list, and appointment book on top of her Bible, with her pencils and pens to the side. And that was how she lived. All of her lists were made and all of her appointments were chosen through the lens of God's desires for her life. The most important preparation Mama made for Sunday mornings was spending time in God's Word *every* morning. She acknowledged her need for God's direction and favor.

When Mama died, their pastor came over to talk to Daddy and us kids. He wanted her funeral to be personal, so he asked us about memories of Mama. We spent a happy couple of hours reminiscing and laughing, pondering, and weeping. Yes, weeping was part of the happiness because she was a special Mama.

Each of us shared several stories, but I'll never forget one my brother Winston told. It happened when he was in college, I think, and was home for a break. Over breakfast Mama and Daddy argued about something. They didn't argue often, but still my brother didn't think much of it. But later, when he and my daddy were on the fourth tee at the golf course, they saw Mama walking their way. She had come to the golf course to apologize to Daddy and ask his forgiveness. Of course, Daddy accepted her apology, and then Mama turned around and walked back in the direction of the clubhouse where her car was parked. That act of humility made a deep impression on my brother.

We'll never know for sure, but I think Mama had opened her Bible to have a quiet time of prayer and was convicted that she couldn't worship God until there was nothing unsettled between her and her husband. Maybe she was reading Matthew 5:21-24.

> "You're familiar with the command to the ancients, 'Do not murder.' I'm telling you that anyone who is so much as angry with a brother or sister is guilty of murder. Carelessly call a brother 'idiot!' and you just might find yourself hauled into court. Thoughtlessly yell 'stupid!' at a sister and you are on the brink of hellfire. The simple moral fact is that words kill.

> "This is how I want you to conduct yourself in these matters. If you enter your place of worship and, about to make an offering, you suddenly remember a grudge a friend has against you, abandon your offering, leave immediately, go to this friend and make things right. Then and only then, come back and work things out with God."

So perhaps another thing wrong with our Sunday mornings is that we have wounds, jealousies, grudges, pride issues, or other blood clots in the arteries of our worship. I don't know about you but I sometimes need to humble myself before my friends, loved ones, or observers before I appear before God. Humbled is the best way to worship. Humbled reminds me of who I am and who He is. Humbled brings the breath of heaven down. And what joy follows!

I remember well the day I realized my name and my concerns were on that list on top of Mama's Bible. She prayed for me every morning (and probably at times during the day, too, especially during some seasons of my life). She shared with me that one daily prayer was for God to heal my brain damage. I'm sure she prayed for me to find a godly man. But now that I'm a mom with grown children of my own, I think I know some other things Mama prayed.

- That I would come to my own faith in God.

- That I would use my spiritual gifts.

- That I could learn to love people as Jesus does.

- That I would find my way through the tuggles of life. Tuggles are temptations or struggles or a mixture of both. Think about it. You've been there. Satan loves tuggles because he yearns to enslave us.

I've learned that the tuggles can be what's wrong with our Sunday mornings. If we ever find ourselves thinking *Church is such a drag. I wish I didn't have to go mingle with those hypocrites,* or *I don't feel like praising the Lord, especially with the music we've been singing,* or *The sermons lately - ugh.* If we catch ourselves with those kinds of thoughts or feelings, there must be a tuggle or two or ten, so we should ask ourselves, "What's really going on here?"

Here's what's going on: We're trying to run our races wearing backpacks full of boulders. Some of the boulders are unconfessed sin. Others are frustrations or disappointments of life. A few are unknowns: what ifs, when wills, how cans. All of these things affect our joy in communion with God in burdensome, whiny, itchy sorts of ways. The only way to bring joy back to worship is to unload those heavy or cumbersome backpacks:

- Ask God to show us the sin in our lives, and then agree with Him that it is sin (confess).

115

- Allow God to spread out the maps of our frustrations or disappointments and then smooth them with His powerful hand. I love Babbie Mason's song, "Trust His Heart." Here is the first part:

  > All things work for our good
  > Though sometimes we don't see
  > How they could
  > Struggles that break our hearts in two
  > Sometimes blind us to the truth...
  > God is too wise to be mistaken
  > God is too good to be unkind
  > So when you don't understand
  > When you don't see His plan
  > When you can't trace His hand
  > Trust His Heart.

  > *Babbie Mason/Eddie Carswell © Warner Chappell Music, Inc., Concord Music Publishing LLC

- Give the what ifs, when wills, and how cans to God. Hand them over. In fact, cast them on Him ("Cast all your anxiety on Him because He cares for you." 1 Peter 5:7).

- Take off the backpack. Don't even let its small weight hold us back from joyfully, faithfully, and freely worshiping our good, good Father.

*I remember Mama making these, but I don't remember when she'd have them. They'll make a yummy addition to breakfast, brunch, lunch, or supper

Fried Apples

1 Granny Smith apple per person, cored and then sliced with skin on
1 tsp. sugar per apple
cinnamon
1 tsp. butter per apple

Put sliced apples in a large bowl. Add sugar. Sprinkle liberally with cinnamon. Stir. Melt butter in skillet. Add apple mixture. Cook and stir until apples soften.

"Looks like Ned!"

Don't know who Ned was, but he must've been an ugly dude. If a cake was lopsided, if a dress hung funny or had a loud print, if the choir wasn't arranged tallest in the middle shortest at the ends, or if her hair had bedhead syndrome, Mama would say, "It looks like Ned!"

I just had a thought. Maybe Ned was an acronym. N.E.D. Nearly Eternally Disappointing. Nasty and Excessively Deplorable. Nauseating Everyday Duddiness. Nonstop Excruciatingly Depressing. One could go on and on, but one won't.

The trick to knowing when something or someone "looks like Ned" is having a standard to go by. For example, I have a dress that is very pretty, just the right shade of green to suit my coloring, fits me well, and gets me compliments every time I wear it. So when I go shopping for a new dress and I try on one that doesn't flatter me like that one does, I say to the mirror, "Looks like N.E.D!" Not Ever Doable.

I just had another thought (Wow, two in one hour!). How can we keep from having a witness that "looks like Ned?" The standards are right there in the Scriptures. When Jesus gave His disciples the charge to go tell the nations, He asked them to wait for something.

> On one occasion, while he was eating with them, he gave them this command: "Do not leave Jerusalem, but wait for the gift my Father promised, which you have heard me speak about. For

John baptized with water, but in a few days you will be baptized with the Holy Spirit."… you will receive power when the Holy Spirit comes on you; and you will be my witnesses in Jerusalem, and in all Judea and Samaria, and to the ends of the earth." (Acts 1:4-5, 8)

So the number one way to have a pure, glowing testimony is to be filled with the Holy Spirit and rely on Him to empower and guide us. I can attest that when I rely on my own plans and thoughts, it becomes about me, and frankly, Nigh Entirely Disastrous.

Only through the presence and power of the Holy Spirit can I attain the other standards for witness described in the Bible.

For the Spirit God gave us does not make us timid, but gives us power, love and self-discipline. (2 Timothy 1:7)

Be imitators of God, as beloved children. And walk in love, as Christ loved us and gave himself up for us, a fragrant offering and sacrifice to God. (Ephesians 5:1-2)

Who is going to harm you if you are eager to do good? But even if you should suffer for what is right, you are blessed. "Do not fear their threats; do not be frightened." [Is. 8:12] But in your hearts revere Christ as Lord. Always be prepared to give an answer to everyone who asks you to give the reason for the hope that you have. But do this with gentleness and respect, keeping a clear conscience, so that those who speak maliciously against your good behavior in Christ may be ashamed of their slander. For it is better, if it is God's will, to suffer for doing good than for doing evil. (1 Peter 3:13-17)

Filled with the Spirit. Courageous. Loving. Gentle. Respectful. Self-disciplined. These are standards for a Not-Ned witness.

❧

They say you learn something new every day. My today's education consisted of learning that I am an "extroverted introvert." Sounds ridiculous, but it's a real thing. I always thought I was an introvert who tried to make myself be more extroverted when necessary, but I never really was convinced I had succeeded. Well, I can't claim "success," because what I was doing is what an extroverted introvert does, evidently. She is a person who loves people but needs and guards her alone time to recharge. Who hates small talk (I always called it "gossip," no offense intended, extroverts). Who can be very friendly but just can't seem to nurture friendships like she feels she should. Who can be the life of the party or extremely quiet among a crowd, depending on the day/night. Who, when her social battery is drained, is often misunderstood.

Those who don't know us well are puzzled by our behaviour. If they are around to see us go from fully charged, to depleted, they will usually think one of three things:

a) *Something has happened to make us sad or mad, and it is their duty to fix things by commanding us to "smile", and "stop being a party pooper".*

b) *We hate them, or they have deeply offended us in some way.*

c) *We are silently judging them and the verdict is not good.**

* From "6 Signs You're an Extroverted Introvert," introvertspring.com

So, basically, an onlooker might say our behavior looks like Ned. But it would be a wrong assumption. Hastily judging another person by his or her actions is something we all tend to do. The truth is, relationships are difficult and extremely easy to damage, even without trying. May I make a few suggestions on how to have Not-Ned relationships?

- Give others the benefit of the doubt (translation: Give them a break!). Assume the best intentions. Allow for mistakes.

   I urge you to live a life worthy of the calling you have received. Be completely humble and gentle; be patient, bearing with one another in love. Make every effort to keep the unity of the Spirit through the bond of peace. (Ephesians 4:1-3)

- Forgive and seek forgiveness. Repeat after me: "Even I am wrong sometimes."

   Get rid of all bitterness, rage and anger, brawling and slander, along with every form of malice. Be kind and compassionate to one another, forgiving each other, just as in Christ God forgave you. (Ephesians 4:31-32)

- Strive for unity.

   I pray also for those who will believe in me through their message, that all of them may be one, Father, just as you are in me and I am in you. May they also be in us so that the world may believe that you have sent me. I have given them the glory that you gave me, that they may be one as we are one— I in them and you in me—so that

122

they may be brought to complete unity. Then the world will know that you sent me and have loved them even as you have loved me. (John 17:20-23)

- Laugh. Laugh at yourself. Laugh with others. Loosen up!

  A cheerful heart is good medicine, but a crushed spirit dries up the bones. (Proverbs 17:22)

Our church needs children's choir workers. And Power Point operators. And parking helpers. And preschool Sunday School teachers. And... How surprising. Every church seems to have this same mantra: Help!

Is this anything new? Heavens, no. Mama was the Minister of Music at our church for fifteen years while I was growing up, and I remember her working hard to get and keep choir members. I also remember announcements from the pulpit about workers needed in the nursery or the kitchen or wherever. I learned the miserable truth of the 20/80 rule of most churches. It was true then and is probably true now. Twenty percent of the congregation does eighty percent of the work and gives eighty percent of the money.

What's my point? Let's ask ourselves some questions: *Am I satisfied with attending an hour of church and checking it off my To-Do list? Do I think* 'I've done that already' *or* 'Let someone else do that who has more time than I do'? *Do I believe putting some money in the offering 'pays my way'?* Does our service (or lack thereof) in the ministries of our churches look like Ned?

If it does, maybe we have an erroneous idea of what a church is. It is not a building. Most of us know that. It is not a church service. That may surprise a few. These scriptures will give us an accurate idea of what the church is:

On that day a great persecution broke out against the church in Jerusalem, and all except the apostles were scattered throughout Judea and Samaria. (Acts 8:1)

So for a whole year Barnabas and Saul met with the church and taught great numbers of people. (Acts 11:26)

On arriving there, they gathered the church together and reported all that God had done. (Acts 14:27)

Be shepherds of the church of God, which he bought with his own blood. (Acts 20:28)

Greet also the church that meets at their house. (Romans 16:5)

If I am delayed, you will know how people ought to conduct themselves in God's household, which is the church of the living God, the pillar and foundation of the truth. (1 Timothy 3:15)

A church is a group of believers (the living God's household – Romans 8:14-17) who come together to worship Jesus, to learn more truth about the faith, and to encourage one another in the faith. It takes each one of us to complete the family and to fulfill the mission.

For even the Son of Man did not come to be served, but to serve, and to give his life as a ransom for many. (Mark 10:45)

Then he said to them all: "Whoever wants to be my disciple must deny themselves and take up their cross daily and follow me. (Luke 9:23)

Additionally, God gifted each of us for particular service within the church.

> For we are God's handiwork, created in Christ Jesus to do good works, which God prepared in advance for us to do. (Ephesians 2:10)

> For just as each of us has one body with many members, and these members do not all have the same function, so in Christ we, though many, form one body, and each member belongs to all the others. We have different gifts, according to the grace given to each of us. If your gift is prophesying, then prophesy in accordance with your faith; if it is serving, then serve; if it is teaching, then teach; if it is to encourage, then give encouragement; if it is giving, then give generously; if it is to lead, do it diligently; if it is to show mercy, do it cheerfully. (Romans 12:4-8)

Let's quit this attitude of "church is for me," and discover the Not-Ned gratefulness that looks a lot like hard work and self-denial for the sake of the body of Christ.

Life does not always turn out like we expected, planned, or dreamed it would. Not even the parts that fulfilled romantic fantasies, like marrying the tall, dark, handsome hunkish jock-prince or visiting the castles of Bavaria. My tdhhj-p turned out to be an actual human being who has opinions, generally different from mine. We've somehow made it through forty-three mostly good years in spite of that. And the castles of Bavaria I visited were in beautiful settings and had amazing artwork and architecture. But I didn't really get to live there and experience the "romance" of the Middle Ages.

The highways, back lanes, and ruts of life are mainly unromantic and can sometimes look a lot like Ned. Yet the lows can be overcome and joy can bloom if we look to Jesus. Near the beginning of his ministry, He sat His followers down on a hillside and proceeded to utter some amazing words.

"You're blessed when you're at the end of your rope. With less of you there is more of God and his rule.

"You're blessed when you feel you've lost what is most dear to you. Only then can you be embraced by the One most dear to you.

"You're blessed when you're content with just who you are—no more, no less. That's the moment you find yourselves proud owners of everything that can't be bought.

"You're blessed when you've worked up a good appetite for God. He's food and drink in the best meal you'll ever eat.

"You're blessed when you care. At the moment of being 'care-full,' you find yourselves cared for.

"You're blessed when you get your inside world—your mind and heart—put right. Then you can see God in the outside world.

"You're blessed when you can show people how to cooperate instead of compete or fight. That's when you discover who you really are, and your place in God's family.

"You're blessed when your commitment to God provokes persecution. The persecution drives you even deeper into God's kingdom.

"Not only that—count yourselves blessed every time people put you down or throw you out or speak lies about you to discredit me. What it means is that the truth is too close for comfort and they are uncomfortable. You can be glad when that happens— give a cheer, even!—for though they don't like it, I do! And all heaven applauds. And know that you are in good company. My prophets and witnesses have always gotten into this kind of trouble." (Matthew 5:3-12, The Message)

So mourn, hunger, allow yourself to be humbled and persecuted. Let go of trying to control your life and let God take the Ned parts and use them for His glory.

❧

God saw all that he had made, and it was very good. (Genesis 1:31)

Perfection. It didn't stay that way, did it? Man chose his own way instead of God's way, and bam, evil got ahold of the world. I wouldn't be surprised if God stood back and said, "It looks like Ned!" Actually, he sorta did. Genesis 6:5-7, 13 records:

The Lord observed the extent of human wickedness on the earth, and he saw that everything they thought or imagined was consistently and totally evil. So the Lord was sorry he had ever made them and put them on the earth. It broke his heart. And the Lord said, "I will wipe this human race I have created from the face of the earth... So God said to Noah, "I have decided to destroy all living creatures, for they have filled the earth with violence. Yes, I will wipe them all out along with the earth!"

According to the Bible, man has been insisting on his own way for all of human history. But God continues to pursue His creation because He wants reconciliation and relationship. I find it astonishing yet delightful that even after Jesus had gone back to heaven, He spoke to John through an angel and sent messages to the churches in Asia Minor. He had some complaints about them, complaints He might have about us as well, but He also provided some solutions. He said, "This looks like Ned, but here's what you can do about it." Let's ponder honestly what He's saying to us today.

Read each passage, and fill in the blanks:

Revelation 2:1-5

To the angel of the church in Ephesus write:

These are the words of him who holds the seven stars in his right hand and walks among the seven golden lampstands. I know your deeds, your hard work and your perseverance. I know that you cannot tolerate wicked people, that you have tested those who claim to be apostles but are not, and have found them false. You have persevered and have endured hardships for my name, and have not grown weary.

Yet I hold this against you: You have forsaken the love you had at first. Consider how far you have fallen! Repent and do the things you did at first. If you do not repent, I will come to you and remove your lampstand from its place.

Church: _____

Complaint: _____

Solution: _____

Revelation 2:8-10

"To the angel of the church in Smyrna write:

These are the words of him who is the First and the Last, who died and came to life again. I know your afflictions and your poverty— yet you are rich! I know about the slander of those who say they are Jews and are not, but are a synagogue of Satan. Do not be afraid of what you are about to suffer. I tell you, the devil will put some of you in prison to test you, and you will suffer persecution for ten days. Be faithful, even to the point of death, and I will give you life as your victor's crown.

Church: _____

Complaint: _____

_____

Solution: _____

Revelation 2:14-16

"To the angel of the church in Pergamum write: I have a few things against you: There are some among you who hold to the teaching of Balaam, who taught Balak to entice the Israelites to sin so that they ate food sacrificed to idols and committed sexual immorality. Likewise, you also have those who hold to the teaching of the Nicolaitans. Repent therefore! Otherwise, I will soon come to you and will fight against them with the sword of my mouth.

Church: _____

Complaint:_____

_____

Solution: _____

Revelation 2:20-25

"To the angel of the church in Thyatira write:

I have this against you: You tolerate that woman Jezebel, who calls herself a prophet. By her teaching she misleads my servants into sexual immorality and the eating of food sacrificed to idols. I have given her time to repent of her immorality, but she is unwilling. So I will cast her on a bed of suffering, and I will make those who commit adultery with her suffer intensely, unless they repent of her ways. I will strike her children dead. Then all the churches will know that I am he who searches hearts and minds, and I will repay each of you according to your deeds.

Now I say to the rest of you in Thyatira, to you who do not hold to her teaching and have not learned Satan's so-called deep secrets, 'I will not impose any other burden on you, except to hold on to what you have until I come.'

Church: _____

Complaint:_____

_____

Solution: _____

Revelation 3:1-3

"To the angel of the church in Sardis write:

These are the words of him who holds the seven spirits[b] of God and the seven stars. I know your deeds; you have a reputation of being alive, but you are dead. 2 Wake up! Strengthen what remains and is about to die, for I have found your deeds unfinished in the sight of my God. 3 Remember, therefore, what you have received and heard; hold it fast, and repent. But if you do not wake up, I will come like a thief, and you will not know at what time I will come to you.

Church: _____

Complaint:_____

_____

Solution: _____

Revelation 3:14-19

"To the angel of the church in Laodicea write:

These are the words of the Amen, the faithful and true witness, the ruler of God's creation. I know your deeds, that you are neither cold nor hot. I wish you were either one or the other! So, because you are lukewarm—neither hot nor cold—I am about to spit you out of my mouth. You say, 'I am rich; I have acquired wealth and do not need a thing.' But you do not realize that you are wretched, pitiful, poor, blind and naked. I counsel you to buy from me gold refined in the fire, so you can become rich; and white clothes to wear, so you can cover your shameful nakedness; and salve to put on your eyes, so you can see.

Those whom I love I rebuke and discipline. So be earnest and repent.

Church: _____

Complaint:_____

_____

Solution: _____

- You have left your first love. You have quit doing the deeds you did when you were so excited about being saved.

- You are afraid of persecution, that is, afraid you won't remain faithful.

- You have allowed other gods among you.

- You have tolerated adultery and immorality.

- You have a reputation of being alive, but you are dead. You have unfinished deeds.

- You are lukewarm. You don't realize that you are wretched, pitiful, poor, blind and naked.

Yikes! Does any of that sound familiar? I feel rebuked and humbled. What was Jesus' recommendation? Repent. Do not be afraid. Repent. Repent. Repent. Repent. To repent means to turn and go the opposite direction.

The solution to end all solutions is in verse 20 of chapter 3:

"Here I am! I stand at the door and knock. If anyone hears my voice and opens the door, I will come in and eat with that person, and they with me."

Jesus tells us that repentance happens while we are associating with Him and conversing with Him. Isaiah 1:18 (New King James Version) says,

> "Come now, and let us reason together, says the Lord: though your sins are like scarlet, they shall be as white as snow; though they are red like crimson, they shall be as wool."

Sometimes our hair, cake, or dress is going to "look like Ned." But our hearts, our relationships, our lives, and our service don't have to. Jesus is the answer. Let's turn to Him, believe Him, accept Him, trust Him, imitate Him, lean on Him.

*Mama noted this recipe was from Clara – Charlotte, NC. My taste buds would like to personally thank Clara, whoever she is.

Cheese Biscuits

(aka "Not-Ned Tasty Dainties")
1 cup butter, room temperature
½ pound sharp cheddar, grated (use small grater), room temperature
2 cups flour
½ tsp. salt
1 tsp. paprika
dash (or more) cayenne pepper
pecan halves (75 to 100)

Mix flour, salt, paprika, and cayenne. Mix grated cheese and butter with fingers. Gradually add flour mixture. Roll into marble-sized balls and press each down with a pecan half. Bake at 400 degrees for 10-12 minutes. Cool completely.

"It'll Get Better Before You Get Married"

Back in the sixties, there was no such phrase as "helicopter parent." Parents didn't hover over you. You stayed outside playing until dark or when they called you in for supper or *maybe* when you needed to go to the bathroom. You rode your bike *in the street, without a helmet.* You stood at the bus stop in the freezing cold rain until the bus squeaked up the hill and the door swung out and almost hit you. You ran barefoot all summer long or maybe wore flip flops when you were going to the pool. They dropped you off at the pool, the movies, the fair, and the haunted house. You didn't have a cell phone. You had a dime in your shoe in case of emergency. When you got in trouble at school, your parents didn't go marching up there to yell at the teacher. They yelled at, or in my parents' case - lectured, YOU.

Getting hurt was part of growing up. Skinned knees, burnt fingers, sprained ankles, mosquito bites, bad haircuts, unrequited puppy love, not getting the exact Christmas present you wanted or grade you expected – all these were big, colorful, painful blotches in the paintball game called life. And when I moaned or groaned or cried or complained, Mama would declare, "It'll get better before you get married." And she was right. It did. My knee healed, my hair grew, my heart mended, I forgot about the Christmas present. Even the biggest hurts came into perspective over time.

God isn't in the business of hurting us or letting us get hurt just for the fun of it. In fact, He says,

> "For I know the plans I have for you," declares the Lord, "plans to prosper you and not to harm you, plans to give you hope and a future." (Jeremiah 29:11)

However, do you know your Bible history? These words by Jeremiah were spoken to the people Nebuchadnezzar had conquered in Jerusalem and carried off to exile in Babylon. God had allowed them to be hurt because they had rejected Him and worshiped idols. He had warned them of the coming exile, but they had not confessed or repented or seemed to care. So He sent the Babylonian army to annihilate most of the Israelites. The remnant who were left alive were transported to a land far away. Still, God promised that it would get better. And it did. After seventy years of captivity, the Israelites were freed to return to their own land. And God did all of this for one reason – that they would know that He was the Lord (see Ezekiel 6:14, 7:4, 9, 27).

God's ultimate plan is for our hope and His glory.

> [18] I consider that our present sufferings are not worth comparing with the glory that will be revealed in us. 19 For the creation waits in eager expectation for the children of God to be revealed.

> [20] For the creation was subjected to frustration, not by its own choice, but by the will of the one who subjected it, in hope

> [21] that the creation itself will be liberated from its bondage to decay and brought into the freedom and glory of the children of God...

> [28] And we know that in all things God works for the good of

those who love him, who have been called according to his purpose...

[31] If God is for us, who can be against us? [32] He who did not spare his own Son, but gave him up for us all—how will he not also, along with him, graciously give us all things? (Romans 8, selected verses)

For our light and momentary troubles are achieving for us an eternal glory that far outweighs them all. So we fix our eyes not on what is seen, but on what is unseen, since what is seen is temporary, but what is unseen is eternal. (2 Corinthians 4:17-18)

Blessed is the one who perseveres under trial because, having stood the test, that person will receive the crown of life that the Lord has promised to those who love him. (James 1:12)

For the Lord himself will come down from heaven, with a loud command, with the voice of the archangel and with the trumpet call of God, and the dead in Christ will rise first. After that, we who are still alive and are left will be caught up together with them in the clouds to meet the Lord in the air. And so we will be with the Lord forever. Therefore encourage one another with these words. (1 Thessalonians 4:16-18)

This will be the marriage of the bride (Christ's church) and the bridegroom (Jesus Christ). Here is what the marriage will look like:

I saw the Holy City, the new Jerusalem, coming down out of heaven from God, prepared as a bride beautifully dressed for her husband. And I heard a loud voice from the throne saying, "Look! God's dwelling place is now among the people, and he will dwell with them. They will be his people, and God himself will be with them and be their God. 'He will wipe every tear from their eyes. There will be no more death' or mourning or crying or pain, for the old order of things has passed away." He who was seated on the throne said, "I am making everything new!" Then he said, "Write this down, for these words are trustworthy and true." (Revelation 21:2-5)

I thought Mama was being silly, but I guess she was almost right. It'll definitely get better *when* we get married!

We will be better in the New Jerusalem under the rule of the righteous king Jesus, forever in His presence living in the light of His glory. But what about until then? Earlier I said that even my biggest hurts came into perspective over time. People say that time heals all wounds, but I have found that what time does is give you a different perspective. And if you give your wounds to God, He can give you an eternal perspective that surpasses the ordinary time and space perspective of this world.

Jesus said, "In this world you will have trouble, but take heart! I have overcome the world" (John 16:33). This reassurance is just a small part of a speech filled with comfort and encouragement found in John 14-16. Jesus and His disciples are in the upper room where they've shared the Passover meal and He has washed their feet. Then He predicts that one of them will betray Him and that Peter will deny Him. The disciples are confused, dismayed, and a little afraid of the future. Though they have been with Jesus for three years, they still do not understand about His suffering and what it will mean.

Jesus knows they're scared, and He says, "Don't be troubled." The

Message puts it this way: "Don't let this throw you."

Have you been wounded by fear? In other words, does fear of the unknown paralyze you and keep you from living a victorious life? It'll get better before you get married if you will look at fear from God's perspective. Ask yourself these questions:

What's the worst that could happen to me?

You *will* have troubles. Read your bible. Every major character had troubles. Some even died as a result of their troubles (i.e. John the Baptist, Matthew 14:1-12).

Who has overcome death (overcome the world)?

Christ overcame death, which doesn't mean we don't experience the death of our physical bodies. What it means is that through trusting in Christ, our spirits never die. When our physical bodies die, our spirits are "absent from the body and present with the Lord" (2 Corinthians 5:8). That is why Paul said, "For me, living means living for Christ, and dying is even better" (Philippians 1:21, NLT).

Who is for me?

So dying is better, but we have to live in this fallen world, and it's hard. It helps if you have someone who is for you. Perhaps you can list a bunch of people who are on your side. They root for you. Maybe they even pray for you. When you are fighting fear, they lift your name up to Jesus because, though they are for you, they are not powerful enough to march against the source of fear. "God has not given us a spirit of fearfulness, but one of power, love, and sound judgment" (2 Timothy 1:7, HCSB). Satan is the giver of fear, and the only One who is powerful enough to stand against him is God.

Here's the great news, friends: The almighty God of the universe is for us (you and me). "If God is for us, who can be against us?" (Romans 8:31)

If I've got my God on my side, what am I afraid of?

We find the account of Gideon in Judges 6 – 8. The Midianites were terrorizing Israel at this time, and Gideon was hiding in a winepress to thresh his wheat when an angel of the Lord appeared to him and said, "The Lord is with you, mighty warrior." Gideon was skeptical. His response was, "The Lord is with us?? Then why are we suffering like this?" (my paraphrase)

God then says "Go with the strength you have, and rescue Israel from the Midianites. I am sending you!"

Gideon thinks, as we often do, of his own strength, which isn't much. But God named him Mighty Warrior and gave him His strength. When God says to us, "I am sending you," the emphasis is on "I" and not on "you."

Gideon still balks because his focus is on himself. Fear does that to us. All we can think of is our lack. Gideon needs to focus on God's promise. His word is true and sure. "**I** will be with you. The Midianite army will seem like one man as **I** empower you to defeat them" (my paraphrase of verse 16). God is saying to Gideon and He says to us, "If I am on your side, what do you have to fear?"

> "The Lord is my shepherd; I shall not want…Even though I walk through the valley of the shadow of death, I will fear no evil, for you are with me;…" (Psalm 23:1 and 4, ESV)

The phrase "Do not be afraid" appears 70 times in the NIV. Notice

140

that God doesn't say, "There's nothing to be afraid of." Life can be scary, but He says, "Do not be afraid" because He is more powerful than the ruler of the world. In fact, the "Do not be afraid" phrase is often followed by an action God will take, such as "Do not be afraid of them; the Lord your God himself will fight for you" (Deuteronomy 3:22).

Notice also that God doesn't say, "Why don't you try not being afraid for awhile? You might like it." Instead, his words are a command: "Do not be afraid." And we can obey him because He is trustworthy. He has overcome death. He is with us and is for us.

It'll get better before you get married if you will trust God and His purposes rather than inviting fear in to cripple your spirit.

A wound of fear can paralyze you, but there's another wound that will poison you – the wound of hatred. Every one of us has experienced adversity, both from life and from the people in our lives. The renowned cartoonist Charles Schulz once said, "I love mankind; it's people I can't stand." The idea of loving others unconditionally is splendid. It's the doing of it that takes a godly perspective and the Holy Spirit's power. It's so much easier to get mad and go home. And stay mad and become bitter. And rot in your own skin while blaming the other person.

The world and our sin natures tell us, "You deserve to be angry. You are justified in hating her." But Jesus' teaching is just the opposite: "You have heard that it was said, 'Love your neighbor and hate your enemy.' But I tell you, love your enemies and pray for those who persecute you, that you may be children of your Father in heaven… If you love those who love you, what reward will you get? Are not even the tax collectors doing that? And if you greet only your own people, what are you doing more than others? Do not even pagans do that?" (Matthew 5:43-44, 46-47)

Earlier in that sermon Jesus had said,

> "You have heard that it was said, 'Eye for eye, and tooth for tooth.' But I tell you, do not resist an evil person. If anyone slaps you on the right cheek, turn to them the other cheek also. And if anyone wants to sue you and take your shirt, hand over your coat as well. If anyone forces you to go one mile, go with them two miles" (Matthew 5:38-41).

Another time, Peter asked Jesus, "Lord, how many times shall I forgive my brother or sister who sins against me? Up to seven times?" Jesus answered, "I tell you, not seven times, but seventy-seven times" (Matthew 18:21-22).

What if we refuse to let anger and hate consume us? What if instead we pray for the people who hurt us, anger us, steal from us, or oppress us? What if we choose forgiveness, like Jesus did? When He was dying on the cross and uttered, "Father, forgive them, for they know not what they do," He didn't mean they didn't know they were crucifying Him or that they didn't know He was innocent. He meant they didn't realize how hard their hearts were and what the consequences would be. Often, when someone commits a sin against us, she doesn't comprehend the wound she's inflicting or how hard her heart must have become. We need to have compassion on those who act out of hard hearts and not let our own hearts become hard in response.

Paul wrote to the church at Corinth,

> "The very fact that you have lawsuits among you means you have been completely defeated already. Why not rather be wronged? Why not rather be cheated?" (1 Corinthians 6:7)

It'll get better before you get married if you will let God avenge. Listen to Scripture:

> Beloved, never avenge yourselves, but leave it to the wrath of God, for it is written, "Vengeance is mine, I will repay, says the Lord." (Romans 12:19, ESV)

> Vengeance is mine, and recompense, for the time when their foot shall slip; for the day of their calamity is at hand, and their doom comes swiftly. (Deuteronomy 32:35, ESV)

> Do not say, "I will repay evil"; wait for the Lord, and he will deliver you. (Proverbs 20:22, ESV)

> You shall not take vengeance or bear a grudge against the sons of your own people, but you shall love your neighbor as yourself: I am the Lord.   (Leviticus 19:18, ESV)

"Wherever you go, there you are." – Thomas a Kempis

We can interpret this in two ways. It may mean that you can't run from yourself. That no matter how hard you might try to escape your life, that you will have to change or your life will be the same wherever *you* are? Or it might mean that wherever you let your thoughts go, you'll end up in that place, be it a better place or a worse one.

Either interpretation will go with what I'm saying today, and that is that we frequently carry around the wound of misunderstanding. Misunderstanding can occur through words, unsaid words, actions, or assumptions. How many times do we experience in reality this quote by Alan Greenspan: "I know you think you understand what you thought I said but I'm not sure you realize that what you heard is not what I meant"? If we don't pursue understanding by asking for further explanation, if instead we assume we know, we are more apt to get fearful, feel hurt, get angry, or perhaps judge that person wrongly.

Oops, and wherever we've let our minds go, there we are. In a rut of fear or anger or being judgmental. We've ended up somewhere we didn't intend to be, but once there, we have a hard time getting back to where we want to be.

Judging others doesn't always stem from misunderstanding them, but misunderstanding others can frequently lead to judging them. For instance, I think I know what a person believes, so I judge her choices. Or I'm sure I know someone's motives, so I judge his actions. Maybe I heard only part of a conversation or saw only a bit of an interaction, but I decide the person is greedy, hateful, biased, crazy, etc. It's like I'm training for the jumping to conclusions event at the Olympics.

While I hope you're smiling, I also hope you're thinking about your habits, because becoming a judgmental person is as easy as sliding on pine straw. Down you go, and frequently you don't even realize you've become so self-righteous. The Pharisees were like this. Their primary purpose, it seems, was to condemn others, thus elevating

144

themselves. They avoided self-examination and repentance, and that's why Jesus said,

> "Do not judge, or you too will be judged. For in the same way you judge others, you will be judged, and with the measure you use, it will be measured to you.
>
> "Why do you look at the speck of sawdust in your brother's eye and pay no attention to the plank in your own eye? How can you say to your brother, 'Let me take the speck out of your eye,' when all the time there is a plank in your own eye? You hypocrite, first take the plank out of your own eye, and then you will see clearly to remove the speck from your brother's eye.
>
> "Do not give dogs what is sacred; do not throw your pearls to pigs. If you do, they may trample them under their feet, and turn and tear you to pieces." (Matthew 7:1-6)

Isaiah 33:22 tells us, "For the Lord is our judge; the Lord is our lawgiver; the Lord is our king; ..." James 4:12 reminds us, "There is only one lawgiver and judge, he who is able to save and to destroy. But who are you to judge your neighbor?" And Paul made it clear that we would all be judged by the righteous judge: "For we must all appear before the judgment seat of Christ, so that each one may receive what is due for what he has done in the body, whether good or evil" (2 Corinthians 5:10).

Jesus' command not to judge doesn't mean we cannot show discernment. In fact, when He goes on to say, "Do not give dogs what is sacred; do not throw your pearls to pigs," He was telling His followers not to waste their breath sharing the gospel with those who had already rejected it. In order to heed Jesus' message, they would have had to judge whether someone was open to the gospel or not.

Gotquestions.org further explains this passage:

> Also, the Bible's command that we not judge others does not mean all actions are equally moral or that truth is relative. The Bible clearly teaches that truth is objective, eternal, and inseparable from God's character. Anything that contradicts the truth is a lie—but, of course, to call something a "lie" is to pass judgment. To call adultery or murder a sin is likewise to pass judgment—but it's also to agree with God. When Jesus said not to judge others, He did not mean that no one can identify sin for what it is, based on God's definition of *sin*.

What Jesus meant was that superficial judgment, hypocritical judgment, harsh judgment, and self-righteous judgment are wrong. It'll get better before you get married if instead of becoming a judgmental person you grow up in your faith as Titus 3:1-5 commands:

> Remind your people to submit to rulers and authorities, to obey them, and to be ready to do good in every way. Tell them not to speak evil of anyone, but to be peaceful and friendly, and always to show a gentle attitude toward everyone. For we ourselves were once foolish, disobedient, and wrong. We were slaves to passions and pleasures of all kinds. We spent our lives in malice and envy; others hated us and we hated them. But when the kindness and love of God our Savior was revealed, he saved us. It was not because of any good deeds that we ourselves had done, but because of his own mercy that he saved us, through the Holy Spirit, who gives us new birth and new life by washing us.

When Mama said, "It'll get better before you get married," it was usually about something pretty small. When I had a bigger booboo, like the time I fell off my bike and scraped half my lower leg off, she took more drastic measures. Merthiolate. It was red and burned like I can't even describe. It was supposed to prevent infection, but it turns out that it was a compound made of mercury and sodium, so it was banned in the 1990s. Lucky for my children and their children. Whew! I sweat just thinking about it.

Merthiolate was banned because it was toxic. In some cases, it even hindered healing. In other cases, long term effects like decreased urine output, drooling, extreme difficulty breathing, mouth sores, and memory problems occurred. If I hadn't sucked it up many a time I was hurt because I didn't want to suffer the Merthiolate cure, no telling what kind of physical issues I'd have now.

How I wish we could ban the toxin of comparison. When we mistakenly think every aspect of life is a contest, we spend our precious days comparing ourselves to everyone else. Being the best or having the most becomes our primary goal, and the long-term side effects of trying to achieve that goal are serious and habit-forming. Gossip, resentment, being judgmental, and being a mean girl are just a few of the byproducts of a life of comparison, and they are diametrically opposed to God's plan for us.

The following verses give a glimpse of what God wants for us. Can you identify the theme?

> When the Lord restored the fortunes of Zion, we were like those who dreamed.
>
> Our mouths were filled with laughter, our tongues with songs of joy.

147

Then it was said among the nations, "The Lord has done great things for them."

The Lord has done great things for us, and we are filled with joy. (Psalm 126:1-3)

She is clothed with strength and dignity; she can laugh at the days to come. (Proverbs 31:25)

All the days of the oppressed are wretched, but the cheerful heart has a continual feast. (Prov. 15:15)

You make known to me the path of life; you will fill me with joy in your presence, with eternal pleasures at your right hand. (Psalm 16:11)

Let all those that seek thee rejoice and be glad in thee. (Ps. 40:16a)

I have told you this so that my joy may be in you and that your joy may be complete. (John 15:11)

We write this to make our joy complete. (1 John 1:4)

Life is tough. It's not fair. There are days when you feel you can't win for losing. You can't control the weather, the stock market, what other people think, or even yourself from time to time. You could spend your whole life crying over stuff, being afraid of stuff, holding grudges, and comparing your life to another's. But we were made for more than that. We were made for joy and love and laughter. Mama often said, "You might as well laugh as cry."

So I'm challenging you to let go of negativism in the form of fear, hatred, judgmentalism, and jealousy. I'm urging you to choose joy. Let it be your theme whether the day is bright or stormy, whether the people around you are genuine or phony, whether your boss is grateful or hateful, whether the news is inspiring or disheartening,

148

whether someone gave you a generous compliment or a hurtful criticism. Choose joy – the knowledge that in this world we will have tribulation, but Jesus has overcome the world. And when you do, it'll be better before you get married.

*There's no note on this one, but I think Mama got this recipe from me. It's definitely "joy" food!

Hot Chicken Salad Au Gratin

2 cups cooked chicken (I use 2 12.5 oz cans of white chicken meat)
2 tsp minced onion
1 cup mayonnaise
1 cup diced celery
1 small can sliced water chestnuts
2 tsp lemon juice
½ cup sliced almonds
1 cup grated cheddar cheese
1 cup crushed potato chips

Mix all ingredients except cheese and potato chips in greased 9 x 13 dish. Top with cheese and then potato chips. Bake at 350 degrees for 20 minutes.

*This can be made a day ahead. Add chips just before baking.

"I'm Just Telling You How the Cow Ate the Cabbage"

I never actually heard my mother say this, but my older sister, who argued with Mama often, heard it a number of times. Anne just couldn't keep her mouth shut, no matter the consequences. Meanwhile, I watched those consequences play out and decided that if I had anything rebellious to say, I would say it quietly into my pillow in the privacy of my bedroom. Yep. My pillow knew I hated Mama when no one else had a clue.

But here's how it would go with Anne, I suspect. Mama would say something Anne didn't want to hear. Anne would then argue the point, and Mama would repeat the unwelcome truth. On the third go around, Mama would say, "Anne, I'm just telling you how the cow ate the cabbage" (This is just how it is, and you might as well accept it).

Sometimes parents, bosses, teachers, and preachers just have to tell people how the cow ate the cabbage. It might not be popular or politically correct, but the truth is the truth whether people want to hear it or not. I've been on the receiving end of this, and I expect you have, too. We often make a joke of it by saying, "Ouch! She's stepping on my toes" or "He stopped preaching and went to meddling!" Or we try to ignore our sin or excuse it by saying, "That's just the way I am."

The thing about biblical truth is this: We can't just ignore it. Ignoring it is essentially a choice to reject it, and there are consequences. A good example is Saul (Paul). He was a devout Jew, a "Hebrew of Hebrews," a zealous Pharisee, a rule-follower (see Philippians 3:5-6). Then he started hearing the disciples preach about Jesus. They were saying things he'd never heard before, things that contradicted what he'd always believed. They were stepping on his toes! He chose to reject the truths they were advocating, but being a zealous man, he couldn't merely walk away. He made it his life purpose to pursue Christians as criminals and to persecute them. Then one day something extraordinary happened. Listen to it in Paul's own words:

> "On one of these journeys [to arrest Christians] I was going to Damascus with the authority and commission of the chief priests. About noon, as I was on the road, I saw a light from heaven, brighter than the sun, blazing around me and my companions. We all fell to the ground, and I heard a voice saying to me in Aramaic, 'Saul, Saul, why do you persecute me? It is hard for you to kick against the goads.'

> "Then I asked, 'Who are you, Lord?'

> "'I am Jesus, whom you are persecuting,' the Lord replied. 'Now get up and stand on your feet. I have appeared to you to appoint you as a servant and as a witness of what you have seen and will see of me. I will rescue you from your own people and from the Gentiles. I am sending you to them to open their eyes and turn them from darkness to light, and from the power of Satan to God, so that they may receive forgiveness of sins and a place among those who are sanctified by faith in me.'" (Acts 26:12-18)

What did Jesus mean when He said, "It is hard for you to kick against the goads"? A goad was a wooden oxen prod with a sharp metal point on one end. The farmer would gently prod the ox with a small prick to keep the ox moving in the right direction. But sometimes the ox would kick back against the goad, and when he did this, the sharp point would stab his leg, causing much greater pain and maybe even injury. Basically, the more an ox kicked, the more he suffered.

Jesus said this is what Paul had done. He had persisted in kicking against the truth of the gospel, causing himself and others much suffering. Then Jesus invited Paul to stand up and change the direction of his life. Jesus promised to tell Paul what to do and then to empower him to do it. Jesus revealed that He would use Paul to reach the Gentiles for the kingdom of God.

Whether Paul accepted it or not, the truth of the gospel was still the truth. He could choose to get on board and be used by God or continue kicking against the goads. Paul decided to choose the truth of the gospel and later penned these words:

> And so it was with me, brothers and sisters. When I came to you, I did not come with eloquence or human wisdom as I proclaimed to you the testimony about God. For I resolved to know nothing while I was with you except Jesus Christ and him crucified. I came to you in weakness with great fear and trembling. My message and my preaching were not with wise and persuasive words, but with a demonstration of the Spirit's power, so that your faith might not rest on human wisdom, but on God's power.
>
> We do, however, speak a message of wisdom among the mature, but not the wisdom of this age or of the rulers of this age, who are coming to nothing. No, we declare God's wisdom, a mystery

that has been hidden and that God destined for our glory before time began. (1 Corinthians 2:1-7)

Listen, I'm just gonna tell you how the cow ate the cabbage. The gospel is true whether we accept it or not. But if we will accept it, God will save us and use us beyond our wildest dreams. So quit kicking, friend.

༝

I know I said Anne sometimes didn't prefer the truths Mama embraced, but to be honest, I didn't always like them either. I didn't often kick verbally, but I sure did kick mentally or in my spirit. I spent many years using plenty of energy trying to disprove some of the basic truths of life and Christianity.

When I was about fifteen, my grandmother Crawley said something to me that I kicked against for years. "God isn't trying to make you happy, Joy. He's trying to make you holy."

Sputter, sputter, hackles rising, *How could you say that? I'm going to look that up in the Bible!* Kicking against the goads.

Okay, here I go again. I'm gonna tell you how the cow ate the cabbage. Have you noticed that life is hard? That life isn't fair? God's main purpose in creating you and me was not to make us happy or comfortable. He made us for relationship with Him. He set us apart (which is the true meaning of the word 'holy') to enjoy us and for us to enjoy Him. Even when our circumstances aren't happy or comfortable. In the midst of the unfairness of life.

Everything He allows into our lives is for the purpose of helping us stay set apart. Everything He doesn't allow is for that purpose as well. And whether we feel it or not, we are blessed, because God is for us. He is making each of us into the image of Christ.

Think about Jesus Christ. We don't know too much about the first thirty years of His life, but here's some of what we do know:

- There was controversy concerning His birth - that whole "a virgin will conceive" thing.

- King Herod wanted to kill Him almost as soon as He was born.

- His family had to move around a good bit until King Herod died.

- His parents accidentally left Him behind in Jerusalem one year when they went to Passover.

Now think about years thirty through thirty-three of Jesus' life.

- His hometown rejected Him.

- His own family didn't believe Him.

- The religious leaders tried over and over to trick Him, accuse Him of blasphemy, and defame Him.

- His own disciples just didn't get Him, no matter how often He explained His purpose.

- People often followed Him only for what they could get from Him.

- He was falsely accused, led to an unfair trial, traded in for a notorious convict, beaten and mocked, crucified like a common criminal, and laid in a borrowed grave.

What part of that was happy, easy, or comfortable? Listen, it was God's pleasure to allow His Son to suffer so that we could be saved, forgiven, and reconciled to Him. Now it is God's pleasure to set us apart and make us into the image of Christ, often by allowing really hard things into our lives. That is why James (one of the half-brothers of Jesus who later believed in Jesus as the promised Messiah) said:

My friends, consider yourselves fortunate when all kinds of trials come your way, for you know that when your faith succeeds in facing such trials, the result is the ability to endure. Make sure that your endurance carries you all the way without failing, so that you may be perfect and complete, lacking nothing. (James 1:2-4, GNT)

The goal is that we might be "perfect and complete, lacking nothing." Not happy. Not necessarily unhappy, but the priority is holiness. And when we get there, we will have joy. Now that's the truth.

A hard truth for Jesus? People often followed Him only for what they could get from Him. Listen:

When they found him back across the sea, they said, "Rabbi, when did you get here?"

Jesus answered, "You've come looking for me not because you

saw God in my actions but because I fed you, filled your stomachs—and for free.

"Don't waste your energy striving for perishable food like that. Work for the food that sticks with you, food that nourishes your lasting life, food the Son of Man provides. He and what he does are guaranteed by God the Father to last."

To that they said, "Well, what do we do then to get in on God's works?"

Jesus said, "Throw your lot in with the One that God has sent. That kind of a commitment gets you in on God's works."

They waffled: "Why don't you give us a clue about who you are, just a hint of what's going on? When we see what's up, we'll commit ourselves. Show us what you can do. Moses fed our ancestors with bread in the desert. It says so in the Scriptures: 'He gave them bread from heaven to eat.'"

Jesus responded, "The real significance of that Scripture is not that Moses gave you bread from heaven but that my Father is right now offering you bread from heaven, the *real* bread. The Bread of God came down out of heaven and is giving life to the world."

They jumped at that: "Master, give us this bread, now and forever!"

Jesus said, "I am the Bread of Life. The person who aligns with me hungers no more and thirsts no more, ever. I have told you this explicitly because even though you have seen me in action, you don't really believe me. Every person the Father gives me eventually comes running to me. And once that person is with me, I hold on and don't let go. I came down from heaven not to follow my own whim but to accomplish the will of the One who sent me.

"This, in a nutshell, is that will: that everything handed over to me by the Father be completed—not a single detail missed—and at the wrap-up of time I have everything and everyone put together, upright and whole. This is what my Father wants: that anyone who sees the Son and trusts who he is and what he does and then aligns with him will enter *real* life, *eternal* life. My part is to put them on their feet alive and whole at the completion of time."

At this, because he said, "I am the Bread that came down from heaven," the Jews started arguing over him: "Isn't this the son of Joseph? Don't we know his father? Don't we know his mother? How can he now say, 'I came down out of heaven' and expect anyone to believe him?"

Jesus said, "Don't bicker among yourselves over me. You're not in charge here. The Father who sent me is in charge. He draws people to me—that's the only way you'll ever come. Only then do I do my work, putting people together, setting them on their feet, ready for the End. This is what the prophets meant when they wrote, 'And then they will all be personally taught by God.' Anyone who has spent any time at all listening to the Father, really listening and therefore learning, comes to me to be taught personally—to see it with his own eyes, hear it with his own ears, from me, since I have it firsthand from the Father. No one has seen the Father except the One who has his Being alongside the Father—and you can see *me*.

"I'm telling you the most solemn and sober truth now: Whoever believes in me has real life, eternal life. I am the Bread of Life. Your ancestors ate the manna bread in the desert and died. But now here is Bread that truly comes down out of heaven. Anyone eating this Bread will not die, ever. I am the Bread—living Bread!—who came down out of heaven. Anyone who eats this Bread will live—and forever! The Bread that I present to the world so that it can eat and live is myself, this flesh-and-blood self."

At this, the Jews started fighting among themselves: "How can this man serve up his flesh for a meal?"

But Jesus didn't give an inch. "Only insofar as you eat and drink flesh and blood, the flesh and blood of the Son of Man, do you have life within you. The one who brings a hearty appetite to this eating and drinking has eternal life and will be fit and ready for the Final Day. My flesh is real food and my blood is real drink. By eating my flesh and drinking my blood you enter into me and I into you. In the same way that the fully alive Father sent me here and I live because of him, so the one who makes a meal of me lives because of me. This is the Bread from heaven. Your ancestors ate bread and later died. Whoever eats this Bread will live always."

He said these things while teaching in the meeting place in Capernaum.

Many among his disciples heard this and said, "This is tough teaching, too tough to swallow." (John 6:25-60, The Message)

Tough truth to swallow. And here's a tough question for each of us:

Do I want the Bread, or do I just want the bread?

&

In three separate discourses recorded in the book of Matthew, Jesus taught a hard truth: rule-following is not the same as holiness. The Pharisees had a problem with this truth. The disciples had a problem with this truth. You and I have a problem with this truth. But Jesus made it clear.

Matthew 5:

- Not only is murder wrong, but just being angry at the person or calling him a fool is wrong. So if you've steered clear of murder but you're harboring anger and bitterness, you are no more holy than the murderer.

- Adultery is wrong, sure. But so is lust. So if you're thinking of a person as a sex object, you haven't passed the holiness test.

- You are commanded to love God and love others. However, loving those who love you is not holiness. Loving those who hate you, forgiving those who persecute you, now that's imitating Me.

Matthew 23 is a sermon of seven woes to the scribes and Pharisees, but these concepts are no less applicable in our lives.

- Woe to you because your false holiness (hypocrisy) disgusts Me and confuses or is repulsive to those who are watching you.

160

- Woe to you, frauds! You claim you are making disciples, but you are making them into hypocrites like you.

- Woe to you who think I hear what you say but don't see what you do. Your word is worth nothing.

- Woe to you who think your tithing is holy while you treat your fellow man with contempt and injustice.

- Woe to you who put on your Sunday faces and Jesus tee shirts but it's all just a show.

- Woe to you who act like you've never done anything wrong yet deep inside you are wormy with greed and selfishness.

- Woe to you who pridefully think you would never have made the mistakes your ancestors made. You are sinners just like they were. You need saving just like they did.

Are you feeling the sting yet? Do you want to put your hands over your ears or kick against the goads? Wait. There's one more passage to think about.

In Matthew 25, Jesus summarized for His disciples what is really important in a Christian's life:

- Feed the hungry, both spiritually and physically.

- Give life-giving water to the thirsty, both spiritually and physically.

- Care for the homeless. Give them a place to stay. Welcome them in your circle.

- Clothe those in need.

- Do what you can for the sick.

- Love those who are in prison.

Unlike with social media, we don't get to decide whether to give these truths a 'Like.' We just need to listen, obey, and pass on the word of truth.

Mama didn't always tell the truth. Whoa! Can you believe I said that? But I'm sure she didn't, because no one does. We all tend to exaggerate, or omit parts we're ashamed of, or shy away from saying something others don't want to hear. But God hates lying. Check out this text from Proverbs:

There are six things the Lord hates, seven that are detestable to him:

- haughty eyes,
- a lying tongue,
- hands that shed innocent blood,
- a heart that devises wicked schemes,
- feet that are quick to rush into evil,
- a false witness who pours out lies
- and a person who stirs up conflict in the community. (Proverbs 6:16-19)

How many of the seven things God detests have to do with lying, deceit, or perhaps slander? Choosing not to tell someone something they would rather not hear is the same as leading them to believe a falsehood. Listen, telling someone how the cow ate the cabbage is not often fun. However, God commands us to do it.

> These are the things you are to do: Speak the truth to each other, and render true and sound judgment in your courts; (Zechariah 8:16)

In his commentary on Zechariah 8, Vernon McGee reminds us that lying has become an accepted part of our lives. Businesses often use deceit. False advertising is rampant. We can't trust the news media, the government (either political party), the military, educators, scientists, or sadly, even some religious groups and charities. I guess we should be okay with that, since we too fudge on the truth at times.

However, in Ephesians 4 Paul urges Christians to get up, grow up, and quit being like the world.

> [1-3] In light of all this, here's what I want you to do. While I'm locked up here, a prisoner for the Master, I want you to get out there and walk—better yet, run!—on the road God called you to travel. I don't want any of you sitting around on your hands. I don't want anyone strolling off, down some path that goes nowhere. And mark that you do this with humility and discipline—not in fits and starts, but steadily, pouring yourselves out for each other in acts of love, alert at noticing differences and quick at mending fences.

> [14-15] No prolonged infancies among us, please. We'll not tolerate babes in the woods, small children who are an easy mark for impostors. God wants us to grow up, to know the whole truth

and tell it in love—like Christ in everything.

[17] And so I insist—and God backs me up on this—that there be no going along with the crowd, the empty-headed, mindless crowd.

[20-24] But that's no life for you. You learned Christ! My assumption is that you have paid careful attention to him, been well instructed in the truth precisely as we have it in Jesus. Since, then, we do not have the excuse of ignorance, everything—and I do mean everything—connected with that old way of life has to go. It's rotten through and through. Get rid of it! And then take on an entirely new way of life—a God-fashioned life, a life renewed from the inside and working itself into your conduct as God accurately reproduces his character in you.

[25] What this adds up to, then, is this: no more lies, no more pretense. Tell your neighbor the truth. In Christ's body we're all connected to each other, after all. When you lie to others, you end up lying to yourself. (The Message)

We need to start speaking the truth in love. Maybe we've gone along with the idea that there are many roads to heaven. Or maybe we've led people to believe that we never struggle with sin. Let's each think about our truthfulness and transparency. If there are people you need to be truthful with, write down their names. I'll write down mine. Beside them, write what you need to tell them. Let's pray and then just go tell them how the cow ate the cabbage.

*Mama got this recipe from me. In case you're wondering, this is really good with Corn and Cheese Squares.

Cow and Cabbage Soup

(originally known as Cabbage Beef Soup)

1 ½ pounds ground beef
1 can diced tomatoes
1 can crushed peeled tomatoes
½ bag shredded cabbage with carrots
1 cup chopped onion
2 ½ cups water (or 2 cups beef broth and ½ cup water)
1 teaspoon salt (or to taste)
1 Tablespoon chili powder
1 can light red kidney beans, drained

Mix tomatoes, cabbage, onion, water, and seasonings in a saucepan and bring to a boil. Lower heat and simmer 20 minutes. While the soup is simmering, brown ground beef and drain it. Add beef to tomato mixture and simmer 20 more minutes. Finally, add beans and heat through.

Family Matters

These five days will be based on things Mama used to say to family or about family on a regular basis.

"Don't Borrow Trouble"

I said this just the other day to my sister. It's 2020. If you're alive in 2020, you know it's been a year of trouble. Wildfires in Australia. Impeachment process in the U.S. The United Kingdom withdrawing from the European Union. Iran shooting down a Ukranian airline killing 176 people. Earthquakes in Turkey and the Caribbean. Locust swarms in East Africa. Murder hornets in Washington state, unrest due to protests, riots, and looting in many U.S. cities. And of course, the Coronavirus, which has caused illness, death, economic recession, sports being halted (the Summer Olympics postponed for a year), a rise in suicides and depression, and all around mayhem. I think Jesus was talking about 2020 when He said, "Take therefore no thought for the morrow: for the morrow shall take thought for the things of itself. Sufficient unto the day is the evil thereof" (Matthew 6:34, KJV).

In other words, "Don't borrow trouble from tomorrow. Today has enough." So this wasn't really Mama's saying; Jesus originated it. He had been talking to His followers about their attitudes towards money and possessions. He knew the human tendency is to hoard, worry, and try to control everything because we don't trust God. He also knew bowing to this inclination makes our lives worse. It steals our moments, our days, our years. That's why He said,

> I am the gate. Those who come in through me will be saved. They will come and go freely and will find good pastures. The thief's purpose is to steal and kill and destroy. My purpose is to give them a rich and satisfying life. (John 10:9-10, NLT)

The image of shepherd and sheep is a very common one in Scripture. Isaiah wrote that all of us like sheep have strayed away; we have left God's paths to follow our own. Several psalms mention that God's people are the sheep of his pasture. And of course, Psalm 23 by David, a shepherd, describes in detail how the Lord is our shepherd.

Jesus commented that the crowds who flocked to him were like sheep without a shepherd. I think we can infer that they were sheep who needed a shepherd. They needed someone to care, to ease their burdens, and to show them how to rest. He had compassion for them, wanting them to find freedom from the law and the worries of this world. So He explained that He was the gate into the pasture where they could have abundant life.

If we go through the gate, Jesus Christ, we enter God's pastures and can feel protected and free within the boundaries of His love. And even though our lives on earth are plagued by disease, natural disasters, relationship problems, money trouble, etc., we don't have to worry about the future because we have a Good Shepherd. He saves us and keeps us. A favorite hymn of mine states,

> When I fear my faith will fail, Christ will hold me fast;
> When the tempter would prevail, He will hold me fast.
> I could never keep my hold through life's fearful path;
> For my love is often cold; He must hold me fast.

He will hold me fast, He will hold me fast; For my Saviour loves me so, He will hold me fast. (Ada Habershon)

So don't borrow trouble. He will hold you fast.

"You have to go to bed so I can get some rest."

I don't remember Mama saying this, but I do remember going to bed really early. Like when my friends were still outside playing during the summer, I was in bed at 7. Like when I could hear the others in my family downstairs watching the Dick Van Dyke show and laughing, I was lying in bed whispering "I hate you, Mama" into my pillow. I don't remember ever asking why I had to go to bed. Seven o'clock was just my bedtime.

So when I got grown, I asked Mama why she made my bedtime so early. I expected her to say that she had read a pediatrician's advice or that she had gone to bed at that hour when she was a child and therefore thought it was the norm. But instead she said, "You had to go to bed so I could get some rest." I laughed out loud because I could identify. I had four little girls, and though they were the joy of my life, they wore me plumb out!

Why are children so exhausting? Well, first of all, they have way more energy than most adults. Second, they have so many questions. "Why?" "Why?" "Why?" And third, they'll call you out if you don't practice what you preach. We were recently eating lunch out with my daughter and her family who don't eat strictly Paleo, but close. My daughter ordered hamburgers for herself and their children, no bun. When my son-in-law ordered his hamburger, the server asked, "No bun?" and he replied, "Oh, I want the bun." My seven-year-old grandson exclaimed, "Daddy! We don't eat bread." Busted!

I wasn't a strong-willed child, but I'm sure I had all three of these qualities, so I'm sure Mama needed some rest. But the truth is, I needed rest, too. My body had to recharge. I think we've forgotten this fact. Modern Americans idolize work and entertainment to the point that rest is our last priority. Most of us need a vacation to recuperate from our vacations.

God appointed the Sabbath to help teach His children to rest. Exodus 1:11-14 tells what their lives were like in Egypt:

> So the Egyptians made the Israelites their slaves. They appointed brutal slave drivers over them, hoping to wear them down with crushing labor. They forced them to build the cities of Pithom and Rameses as supply centers for the king. But the more the Egyptians oppressed them, the more the Israelites multiplied and spread, and the more alarmed the Egyptians became. So the Egyptians worked the people of Israel without mercy. They made their lives bitter, forcing them to mix mortar and make bricks and do all the work in the fields. They were ruthless in all their demands.

It sounds as if they were working nonstop, seven days a week for masters who showed no consideration. No wonder they cried out to God to deliver them. Listen to what God told Moses:

> "I have certainly seen the oppression of my people in Egypt. I have heard their cries of distress because of their harsh slave drivers. Yes, I am aware of their suffering. "So I have come down to rescue them from the power of the Egyptians and lead them out of Egypt into their own fertile and spacious land" (Exodus 3:7-8a).

When the Israelites came out of Egypt, they needed new habits. And they needed to be led to these new habits by God. They had been told what to do for generations, so they were looking for freedom. But they needed freedom with boundaries so they could feel secure and loved. One of the ways God provided this was through the Sabbath. He said, "Remember the Sabbath day, to keep it holy" (Exodus 20:8). Remember, the Hebrew word translated 'holy' means 'set apart.' In other words, the Sabbath, or Sunday for Christians, should be different from our other days. We should slow down, quit striving, and know God.

Unlike Mama, God doesn't ask us to rest because He needs rest. He asks us to rest because He knows we need rest. We need a break from our daily grinds. We need a chance to recover from the strains of work, family, expectations, and hurry. And we need to know and worship Him, because He is worthy of our worship and because He is the source of our strength. He is our loving Father, and spending time in rest brings us closer to Him.

"Remember the Sabbath day, to keep it holy" (Exodus 20:8).

"I Married him for Better or Worse, but not for Lunch."

Oh, Mama. She could be a hoot sometimes. But she wasn't kidding when she said this. My daddy traveled for his job a whole bunch when we kids were young. He might be gone two or three or more weeks at a time. Once, when I was a year old, he had to be gone three months. We were living overseas, and Daddy's job description changed, and he had to come to the States to learn the new ropes. So Mama was in charge at home and had us all on a schedule she could handle.

I think that's why, when Daddy was in town, she said, "You go on to work. I've got things under control here. Don't be coming home at lunch and disturbing the status quo." Well, she didn't say it like that. She said, laughing, "I married you for better or worse, but not for lunch!"

When we think we have things under control, we don't want anyone to mess with our plans, do we? I'm not talking about having some order in our lives. We need order. God is a god of order, so He creates in us a desire for stability. But if I make an idol of order, my craving for stability turns into the need to control everything and everyone. I put my plans and purposes over people.

This practice is the complete opposite of Jesus' mode of operation. Sure He had plans. But people were his focus. The Gospels record case after case of Jesus being interrupted. He was interrupted by ceiling debris falling on his head when He was teaching in a house and looked up to see a man being lowered in front of him! He was interrupted by the sight of a man in a tree watching him. He was interrupted by parents wanting their children blessed. He was interrupted when He was eating. He was interrupted even when He tried to get a moment of solitude to grieve the death of his cousin, John the Baptist. He got in a boat to go away, but the multitudes of people followed him, and He had compassion on them and healed their sick and spoke with them. I love the following account because even an interruption was interrupted, and Jesus remained calm and loving.

> When Jesus returned, that the multitude welcomed Him, for they were all waiting for Him. And behold, there came a man named Jairus, and he was a ruler of the synagogue. And he fell down at

Jesus' feet and begged Him to come to his house, for he had an only daughter about twelve years of age, and she was dying.

But as He went, the multitudes thronged Him. Now a woman, having a flow of blood for twelve years, who had spent all her livelihood on physicians and could not be healed by any, came from behind and touched the border of His garment. And immediately her flow of blood stopped.

And Jesus said, "Who touched Me?"

When all denied it, Peter and those with him said, "Master, the multitudes throng and press You, and You say, 'Who touched Me?' "

But Jesus said, "Somebody touched Me, for I perceived power going out from Me." Now when the woman saw that she was not hidden, she came trembling; and falling down before Him, she declared to Him in the presence of all the people the reason she had touched Him and how she was healed immediately.

And He said to her, "Daughter, be of good cheer; your faith has made you well. Go in peace."

While He was still speaking, someone came from the ruler of the synagogue's *house,* saying to him, "Your daughter is dead. Do not trouble the Teacher."

But when Jesus heard *it,* He answered him, saying, "Do not be afraid; only believe, and she will be made well." [51] When He came into the house, He permitted no one to go in except Peter, James, and John, and the father and mother of the girl. Now all wept and mourned for her; but He said, "Do not weep; she is not dead, but sleeping." And they ridiculed Him, knowing that she was dead.

But He put them all outside, took her by the hand and called, saying, "Little girl, arise." Then her spirit returned, and she arose immediately. (Luke 8:40-55)

I totally understand my mama not wanting to have to plan her day around being home at lunch. And it's okay if we have plans and lists and goals. But let's be like Jesus. He had the words of eternal life, but He realized the interruptions were his ministry. They were golden opportunities for teachable moments, relationship-building, and displaying the power of God. Yes. Let's do that.

One of them, an expert in religious law, tried to trap him with this question: "Teacher, which is the most important commandment in the law of Moses?"

Jesus replied, "'You must love the Lord your God with all your heart, all your soul, and all your mind.' This is the first and greatest commandment. A second is equally important: 'Love your neighbor as yourself.' (Matthew 22:35-39)

I press on to take hold of that for which Christ Jesus took hold of me. (Philippians 3:12)

I beg you to lead a life worthy of your calling, for you have been called by God. (Ephesians 4:1, NLT)

"Decide what kind of relationship you want to have in ten years, and act in a way now that will foster that relationship."

Daddy gave Mama this advice when my sister was making choices directly opposed to what they had taught her. Mama was frustrated, broken-hearted, and concerned, and frankly, her pride was hurt, too. She wanted to lash out, preach, and fix what she perceived was wrong. Instead, she took Daddy's advice, swallowing her opinions and preaching, and she and my sister had a wonderful relationship until the day Mama died.

So when one of my daughters was making choices that bothered me, Mama shared this wise advice. She reminded me that being right is not as important as being full of grace and mercy. I'm grateful I listened, because my daughter and I now have a relationship built on love, respect, and trust.

There are three vital steps in heeding my daddy's wise counsel. First, I must decide. Before anything happens, I make a decision about how I will respond. Psalm 118:24 says, "This is the day the Lord has made; we will rejoice and be glad in it" (NLT). In other words, "We have made a decision to rejoice no matter what this day holds, because the Lord gave us this day as a blessing." When I make a decision to be a certain way or have a particular attitude, the battle's half won.

The second step is to think about what kind of relationship I want to have with a person. Do I want to be right no matter what? Do I want to preserve my pride? Do I want to have the last word? Or, do I want my friend, loved one, or acquaintance to feel loved? Do I want to reap peace? Do I want joy? Do I want to feel relaxed around her because there's nothing unsettled between us? Imagine. Consider. It might be hard to envisage a grown woman when you're in an argument with a fourteen-year-old, but she will, God willing, be twenty-four and thirty-four and forty-four one day. What kind of relationship do you want to have then?

And what about in your marriage? Do you want it to last? Do you really desire the "'til death do us part" scenario? What does that kind of relationship look like? You may have to observe or talk to older couples. Are you willing to swallow your pride and ask for help in casting a vision for your marriage?

Third, act. Do the actions that will produce that relationship. I've got a beautiful example. One of my daughters (a different one than the one mentioned above – I've got four!) was more openly strong-willed than the other three. She and I butted heads all the time when she was two, three, four, five….twelve. Once when she was twelve, I took her to a friend's house for some kind of get together. When she got out of the car, I said, "I'll be back at four to pick you up."

She replied, "Uh, no, you can come around six." To which I replied, "No, I'll be here at four. Be ready." She whined, "Mama, everybody's staying later than that. I'm staying until six!"

I'm sure my words were a little clipped when I declared, "Mrs. Parker said it would be over around four. I can come get you at four, or you can go back home with me right now."

She rolled her eyes, harrumphed, and stomped off towards the house. As I drove angrily back to our house, I prayed, "God, what am I going to do with her!?"

Now some of you are not going to believe this, but I actually heard God's voice say, "Love her, Joy." And from that day I decided to do the actions of love even when I wasn't feeling love towards her. I knew I wanted to have a good relationship with her, and I haven't been sorry for the work it took. It took a change of heart – my heart. It took biting my tongue sometimes. It took trying to understand what a strong-willed teenage girl is experiencing. It took crying and prayer and being disappointed. It took loving her enough to let her fail and being there for her when it happened. But I've never been sorry that I decided to love her. Today, she is one of my best friends.

But God demonstrates his own love for us in this: While we were still sinners, Christ died for us. (Romans 5:8)

Do not be deceived: God cannot be mocked. A man reaps what he sows. (Galatians 6:7)

My dear brothers and sisters, take note of this: Everyone should be quick to listen, slow to speak and slow to become angry, because human anger does not produce the righteousness that God desires. (James 1:19-20)

The end of a matter is better than its beginning, and patience is better than pride. Do not be quickly provoked in your spirit, for anger resides in the lap of fools. (Ecclesiastes 7:8-9)

Indeed, there is no one on earth who is righteous, no one who does what is right and never sins. (Ecclesiastes 7:20)

Humble yourselves, therefore, under God's mighty hand, that he may lift you up in due time. Cast all your anxiety on him because he cares for you. (1 Peter 5:6-7)

Above all, love each other deeply, because love covers over a multitude of sins. (1 Peter 4:8)

Always be humble and gentle. Be patient with each other, making allowance for each other's faults because of your love. (Ephesians 4:2)

"We're spending your inheritance!"

We were far from wealthy when I was growing up. Daddy's whole career was in missions work, so we had a tight budget. As far back as I can remember and until the days they became incapacitated, both Mama and Daddy wrote down every penny they spent, and at the end of each day would check their expenditures against the cash left in their wallets. We lived pretty simply, and they saved money for big items like cars, college, weddings, etc.

By the time they retired, my parents had saved and invested well enough to live comfortably in a nice retirement community. They had a sizeable nest egg that my brother, sister, and I would share at their deaths. So every time they scheduled a trip or bought anything of value, Mama would throw back her head and happily cry, "We're spending your inheritance!" All of us would just grin and say, "Do it!"

They didn't spend it all, and each of us inherited a good amount that we'd have been happy to give back just to have more time with them. Our parents themselves – their faith, joy, and love – were the real wealth we inherited. I think the same can be said for Christians. We have an inheritance, which is well documented in scripture.

In John 14:1-3, Jesus is speaking to his disciples the night before He died.

> "Do not let your hearts be troubled. You believe in God; believe also in me. My Father's house has many rooms; if that were not so, would I have told you that I am going there to prepare a place for you? And if I go and prepare a place for you, I will come back and take you to be with me that you also may be where I am."

178

Jesus told his disciples He was going to prepare a place for them in heaven. We can infer that the inheritance of those who believe in Jesus is heaven. 1 Peter 1:3-5 gives a bit more information about the inheritance:

> Praise be to the God and Father of our Lord Jesus Christ! In his great mercy he has given us new birth into a living hope through the resurrection of Jesus Christ from the dead, and into an inheritance that can never perish, spoil or fade. This inheritance is kept in heaven for you, who through faith are shielded by God's power until the coming of the salvation that is ready to be revealed in the last time.

1. The inheritance can never perish. Unlike everything on earth that is dying, decaying, wearing out, or falling apart, our inheritance will remain whole and everlasting.

2. The inheritance is unspoiled. Untouched by sin. Pure. Incorruptible. Truly perfect.

3. The inheritance will never fade. Gotquestions.org describes it this way: "As creatures of this world, it is hard for us to imagine colors that never fade, excitement that never flags, or value that never depreciates; but our inheritance is not of this world. Its glorious intensity will never diminish."

4. The inheritance is reserved for us. We've got reservations in the new Jerusalem! The Holy Spirit who lives within us guarantees our eternal life in our eternal home.

And you also were included in Christ when you heard the message of truth, the gospel of your salvation. When you believed, you were marked in him with a seal, the promised

Holy Spirit, who is a deposit guaranteeing our inheritance until the redemption of those who are God's possession—to the praise of his glory. (Ephesians 1:13-15)

What a promise! What a hope we have! What a day that will be! I'm so excited. But just like with my parents, the treasure is not just eternal life in an incorruptible setting. It's the relationship, the eternity with Christ my Redeemer. But I can experience the gift of that joy and love right now, in the present, every day. It makes me a wealthy, secure person, as described in Psalm 112:1-7 (below).

Praise the Lord.

Blessed are those who fear the Lord,
     who find great delight in his commands.

Their children will be mighty in the land;
     the generation of the upright will be blessed.
Wealth and riches are in their houses,
     and their righteousness endures forever.
Even in darkness light dawns for the upright,
     for those who are gracious and compassionate and righteous.
Good will come to those who are generous and lend freely,
     who conduct their affairs with justice.

Surely the righteous will never be shaken;
     they will be remembered forever.
They will have no fear of bad news;
     their hearts are steadfast, trusting in the Lord.

Grandma's Pineapple Marshmallow Salad

(Ambrosia was the magical fruit of the gods in ancient Greek mythology. I inherited this version from Grandma Lawrence, and it brings back magical memories from my childhood.)

<u>Mayonnaise</u>

2 eggs

2 T. sugar

3 T. vinegar

1 T. flour

Whisk together until completely combined.

<u>Salad</u>

1 cup single cream (whipping cream)

1 cup heavy cream

1 can pineapple tidbits, drained

½ lb. mini marshmallows

Whip mayonnaise and single cream. Add heavy cream and whip until thick. Add marshmallows and pineapple. Chill thoroughly.

Attitude

"It's not just what you say but how you say it."

Words can signify nothing, or they can mean everything. How often do we answer absentmindedly while not really listening? Or perhaps we have said something true but done it in anger or frustration rather than for the sake of helping or reconciliation?

Think about this: The difference between a good actor and a mediocre one or a hilarious comedienne and an unremarkable one is that the great ones know *how* to say the lines so the words make the most impact. Their inflections, their timing, even their body language are important. The same is true for you and me. Our words can mean nothing. We could just be yammering on. But our inflections, our timing, and our body language can convey meaning.

Much of what we say is habitual, either in its content or its intent. Let me share some examples.

After my brother-in-law had a stroke that affected the speech center of his brain, he was able to say the routine sentences such as, "How are you?" and "Hi, there" and "I'm fine" but could not come up with an original sentence. I remember his gesturing towards me and then pointing at his head. I knew he was trying to say he liked my new hairstyle, but all that came from his mouth was gibberish.

Most of us have not had a stroke. Yet often we stick to rote phrases or easy topics of conversation. We may not really listen to what others are trying to say and don't work on ways to truly convey what we are thinking. Instead we murmur, "Uh-huh," or "Oh, really?" or spit out words borrowed from others' ideas or political correctness.

An especially good example of "It's not just what you say but how you say it" is a backhanded compliment. Some people use this hurtful style almost exclusively. You know – a person has something nice to say but something mean to say as well. Consulting.com explains it this way: "When someone pays you a backhanded compliment, you could take it purely as a compliment, and walk away with the glow of receiving a nice comment about your character or appearance. Conversely, you might take it purely as an insult, and walk away with that bitter feeling you get when someone makes a disparaging remark about you. Oftentimes, the receiver can simply end up confused."

- "You look great, *for your age.*"
- "I love your new hairstyle. *It suits you better.*"
- "*I can't believe you're an engineer.* You have to be pretty smart to do that, don't you?"
- "You have such a lovely smile that *people probably don't even notice you're overweight.*"

If this is our mode of speaking, we need to work hard at controlling our jealousy, cattiness, or plain negativity. Our words, tone, and intent show the real state of our hearts.

Solomon understood it:

"Death and life are in the power of the tongue" (Proverbs 18:21).

Paul definitely got it:

> "If I speak in the tongues of men or of angels, but do not have love, I am only a resounding gong or a clanging cymbal" (1 Corinthians 13:1).

> "Do not let any unwholesome talk come out of your mouths, but only what is helpful for building others up according to their needs, that it may benefit those who listen. Get rid of all bitterness, rage and anger, brawling and slander, along with every form of malice. Be kind and compassionate to one another, forgiving each other, just as in Christ God forgave you" (Ephesians 4:29, 31-32).

> "...speaking the truth in love, we will grow to become in every respect the mature body of him who is the head, that is, Christ" (Ephesians 4:15).

And so did James:

> "My dear brothers and sisters, take note of this: Everyone should be quick to listen, slow to speak and slow to become angry" (James 1:19).

Mama must've known that if everyone would slow down and consider how their words sound to others, relationships would be better, and in fact, we'd have a far better world. Mama was a smart woman.

"Get off your high horse."

We've all known someone who was "too big for her britches" (another of Mama's favorites). A know-it-all. Prideful. Thinking she's "all that." Well, if I ever got to thinking I knew more than she did, Mama would say, "Get down off your high horse, young lady!"

Sometimes other people put us on a pedestal, but sometimes we put ourselves there. Way up there on a high horse that's taller than anyone else's, where people can see us and we can lord it over them. Jesus wasn't like that. He came not to be served but to serve (Mark 10:45). He came not to condemn us but to lay down his life for us (John 3:17). He had every right to be on a high horse, but He chose to bend down to help humanity instead (Philippians 2:6-8).

When an expert in the Mosaic law asked Jesus what he could do to inherit eternal life, Jesus asked him, "What does the law say?"

The man replied, " 'Love the Lord your God with all your heart and with all your soul and with all your strength and with all your mind'; and, 'Love your neighbor as yourself.'"

Jesus said, "Okay. Do it."

But then the man, wanting to justify his own attitudes, questioned, "Who is my neighbor?"

That's when Jesus told the parable of the Good Samaritan. You know it: A man was traveling and robbers attacked him, leaving him beaten almost to the point of death. Two religious men saw the injured man but walked on by. A third man, a Samaritan (mixed race, highly detested, often pagan), stopped to help. He cleaned and bandaged the beaten man, took him to an inn, and paid the innkeeper to care for the man until he returned.

Jesus asked, "Which of the three who saw the man acted like a neighbor to him?"

Of course, the answer was the Samaritan. Jesus was making the point that every person, no matter who he is or what we think of him, is equally as important as we are, and we should treat him as significant and valuable. If I don't see other people this way and give of myself to help them, then I'm on my high horse, and I need to get down.

> Therefore, as God's chosen people, holy and dearly loved, clothe yourselves with compassion, kindness, humility, gentleness and patience. Bear with each other and forgive one another if any of you has a grievance against someone. Forgive as the Lord forgave you. And over all these virtues put on love, which binds them all together in perfect unity. (Colossians 3:12-14)

> "For all those who exalt themselves will be humbled, and those who humble themselves will be exalted." (Luke 14:11)

> Humility is the fear of the LORD; its wages are riches and honor and life. Proverbs 22:4)

> Live in harmony with one another. Do not be proud, but be willing to associate with people of low position. Do not be conceited. (Romans 12:16)

"Don't Get Your Back Up"

This saying of Mama's comes from the image of a cat with an arched back, angry and ready to pounce. It simply means, "Don't get angry about this." Sometimes anger is warranted. Jesus got angry when He saw how people were using the temple courts to make money, often cheating the crowds who came to worship. There are times when getting your back up is appropriate, and Jesus' anger here was justified. It was righteous anger.

Most of the time, though, when we're tempted to get offended and angry, it is over our pride. Rather than discuss reasonably our opposing views, we all just get our backs up. This is especially true in our culture these days. I think Mama would've said, "Don't get your backs up. Calm down. Breathe deeply. Take a minute or longer to analyze how your words will sound and what they will say about who you are. Make sure your actions reflect Jesus. Remember that you are a witness, either for Jesus or against Him."

Social media is great for many things, but it is also too easy to say or share something in anger that we'll regret later and forever. I've pretty much quit Facebook because it seemed everyone just had her back up all the time. I honestly was ashamed of what some people who claim to be Christians were posting. I realized that I sort of got my back up over their posts. I also became increasingly afraid of "Liking" a post because I couldn't be sure what news sources to believe. I ended up hurting someone I love just by Liking a post that seemed sane and legitimate. I had to decide if being able to share prayer requests with hundreds of people was worth me being upset or uncertain all the time. The answer the Lord gave me was "No."

My precious mother-in-law used to say, "Patience is a virtue; a virtue is a grace. Put them all together and you have a happy face." Not getting our backs up over every little perceived offense is an example of patience that will make us more content people.

Do not be quickly provoked in your spirit, for anger resides in the lap of fools. (Ecclesiastes 7:9)

A gentle answer turns away wrath, but a harsh word stirs up anger. (Proverbs 15:1)

Be completely humble and gentle; be patient, bearing with one another in love. (Ephesians 4:2)

But the fruit of the Spirit is love, joy, peace, patience,.... (Galatians 5:22)

"Don't Have a Hissy Fit"

A hissy fit, or just plain hissy, is a fancy southern name for a tantrum. The term may have come from the hissing and spluttering a person does in such an outburst, or it may be a shortened form of 'hysterical' or 'histrionics.' Though Mama knew the precepts taught in the Bible, she didn't often quote Scripture at me. But if she had, she might have quoted Philippians 2:14 when I started hissying.

"Do everything without complaining and arguing."

If God says, "Do" in his Word, then it is for our good. It is for the strengthening of our faith or for the building of our character or for the preserving of our testimony. Read Philippians 2:12-16 from the Amplified Bible below, and you'll see that I've underlined words that support all three of the above reasons to do everything without having a hissy fit.

[12] So then, my dear ones, just as you have always obeyed [my instructions with enthusiasm], not only in my presence, but now much more in my absence, continue to work out your salvation [that is, cultivate it, bring it to full effect, actively pursue spiritual maturity] with awe-inspired fear and trembling [using serious caution and critical self-evaluation to avoid anything that might offend God or discredit the name of Christ].

[13] For it is [not your strength, but it is] God who is effectively at

work in you, both to will and to work [that is, strengthening, energizing, and creating in you the longing and the ability to fulfill your purpose] for His good pleasure.

[14] Do everything without murmuring or questioning [the providence of God],

[15] so that you may prove yourselves to be blameless *and* guileless, innocent *and* uncontaminated, children of God without blemish in the midst of a [morally] crooked and [spiritually] perverted generation, among whom you are seen as bright lights [beacons shining out clearly] in the world [of darkness], [16] holding out *and* offering to everyone the word of life,...

Learning to control our thoughts, words, and actions is part of growing up, both emotionally and spiritually. Reading and meditating on God's Word will build a foundation of Christ-control that will be revealed in our self-control.

Better a patient person than a warrior, one with self-control than one who takes a city. (Proverbs 16:32)

But the Holy Spirit produces this kind of fruit in our lives: love, joy, peace, patience, kindness, goodness, faithfulness, gentleness, and self-control. There is no law against these things! (Galatians 5:22-23)

For the Spirit God gave us does not make us timid, but gives us power, love and self-discipline. (2 Timothy 1:7)

Before we close today, let's consider a few more of God's commands to Do, Be, etc. Remember, obeying these will not save you. Only Jesus through his death on the cross can bring you back into relationship with God. But obeying God's commands will bring rich rewards.

Do to others as you would have them do to you. (Luke 6:31)

Be patient with everyone. (1 Thessalonians 5:14b)

Be kind and compassionate to one another, forgiving each other, just as in Christ God forgave you. (Ephesians 4:32)

"Love your enemies! Do good to those who hate you." (Luke 6:27)

"Be careful to do everything I have said to you." (Exodus 23:13a and many other places)

Do not merely listen to the word, and so deceive yourselves. Do what it says. (James 1:22)

So whether you eat or drink, or whatever you do, do it all for the glory of God. (1 Corinthians 10:31)

"Madder Than a Wet Hen"

I didn't know where this phrase originated, so I Googled it. Turns out that hens sometimes enter a phase of "broodiness." They're determined to incubate their eggs and get agitated when the farmer tries to collect the eggs. In order to snap her out of this phase, the farmer will take the hen and dunk her in cold water. She becomes extremely angry but allows the farmer to get her egg. In fact, she may lay even more eggs.

You can imagine the almost comical look and demeanor of this wet hen. Shocked, offended, and completely out of sorts. So if someone is "madder than a wet hen," she has gotten her back up, had a hissy fit, and is now practically smoking out of her ears. It's not attractive. In fact, if you're interested in living another day, you might want to run away from someone who's madder than a wet hen.

In the hen's case, she was just trying to protect her own. She was obeying her instincts, doing what came natural. And along came someone with a cold hand to ruffle her feathers and steal her young. We are often like that hen. We have opinions and ways of doing things that we don't want ruffled. We say, "That's just how I am" or "It's my right…" or "I deserve…."

Remember when my grandmother ruffled my feathers of belief about the happiness I thought I deserved? At first I was madder than a wet hen. But once I began to study the Scriptures and learned she was right, I began to let the Lord calm my heart and He began to mold me. Unfortunately, I didn't immediately set all my thoughts on God's wavelength. Though I was "sanctified [made holy; set apart] through the offering of the body of Jesus Christ once for all" (Hebrews 10:10, KJV), I still sinned. I held onto my pride at times. We all do.

That is why the Bible also speaks of sanctification as a process. God continues to work on me. Philippians 1:6 says, "**God, who began the good work within you, will continue his work until it is finally finished on the day when Christ Jesus returns**" (NLT).

An old song by the Hemphills goes like this:

He's still working on me to make me what I need to be.

It took him just a week to make the moon and the stars,
The sun and the earth and Jupiter and Mars.
How loving and patient he must be,
'Cause he's still working on me.

* Joel Hemphill © Universal Music Publishing Group.

This kind of sanctification comes about through the work of the Holy Spirit applying the Word to our lives. It is sometimes slow work, because we can resist the Holy Spirit. We can continue in pride, stubbornness, immorality, or entitlement. We can reject the truths of Scripture. We can refuse to change. We can brood. It is Christians like this who the world sees as hypocrites. Though we should be looking more and more like Jesus, we are continuing to look like the unsaved.

Sanctification is also hard. That's because our human existence is affected by the fallen world. Our bodies are subject to disease and age. Our minds are bombarded with evil or hurtful ideas almost constantly. These evil and hurtful thoughts then affect our emotions, our relationships, and our ability to move forward. In all this, God wants to heal us and restore us. He wants us to lean into him and find rest. He wants us to align our desires with his desires so that He can make us completely like Jesus. But we have to let him ruffle our feathers and sometimes dunk us in cold water. We have to let go of what we're holding onto and let him have what we hold dear. Our opinions, our "I've always done it this way" attitudes, our "But I don't want to seem odd" fears.

You're cheating on God. If all you want is your own way, flirting with the world every chance you get, you end up enemies of God and his way. And do you suppose God doesn't care? The proverb has it that "he's a fiercely jealous lover." And what he gives in love is far better than anything else you'll find. It's common knowledge that "God goes against the willful proud; God gives grace to the willing humble." (James 4:4-6, The Message)

If we claim to have fellowship with him and yet walk in the darkness, we lie and do not live out the truth. But if we walk in the light, as he is in the light, we have fellowship with one another, and the blood of Jesus, his Son, purifies us from all sin.

If we claim to be without sin, we deceive ourselves and the truth is not in us. If we confess our sins, he is faithful and just and will forgive us our sins and purify us from all unrighteousness. (1 John 1:6-9)

Don't let anyone capture you with empty philosophies and high-sounding nonsense that come from human thinking and from the spiritual powers of this world, rather than from Christ. (Colossians 2:8)

Do not love this world nor the things it offers you, for when you love the world, you do not have the love of the Father in you. For the world offers only a craving for physical pleasure, a craving for everything we see, and pride in our achievements and possessions. These are not from the Father, but are from this world. And this world is fading away, along with everything that people crave. But anyone who does what pleases God will live forever. (1 John 2:15-17)

Dear friends, I warn you as "temporary residents and foreigners" to keep away from worldly desires that wage war against your very souls. Be careful to live properly among your unbelieving neighbors. Then even if they accuse you of doing wrong, they will see your honorable behavior, and they will give honor to God when he judges the world. (1 Peter 2:11-12)

Therefore be imitators of God, as beloved children. (Ephesians 5:1)

Take delight in the Lord, and he will give you the desires of your heart. (Psalm 37:4)

*Mama noted that this recipe came from Better Homes & Gardens magazine. It tastes like home to me because it has an Asian flavor and because Mama always served it on rice, our family's go-to starch when I was growing up.

Meat Patties in Sweet-Sour Sauce

2 cups soft bread crumbs (2-3 pieces of bread)
¼ cup chopped onion and 1 cup sliced onion
1 tsp. salt
½ cup water
1 pound ground beef (or other meat)
Sauce: (I always double this.)
¼ cup brown sugar
1 T. flour
¼ cup vinegar
2 T. water
2 tsp. yellow mustard

Combine crumbs, chopped onion, salt, and water. Let stand 5 minutes. Mix in meat. Shape into patties, then brown in small amount of fat. Drain. Cover patties in sliced onion. Combine brown sugar, flour, vinegar, water, and yellow mustard. Pour over onion slices. Cover and simmer 35 minutes. Serve over rice. Makes 4-5 servings.

Exclamations

Bertha: I saw Jimmy Pate at the grocery this morning.

Mama: You don't mean it!

Bertha: Yep, he told me he's moving back up here to Diggsville next month.

Mama: Well, I'll be! Never thought he'd move back to town.

Bertha: He's got him a new wife. She's the one who talked him into it.

Mama: My stars and garters! Why would she want to move here? Diggsville is just a wide place in the road.

Bertha: I know. But I heard she's trying to buy the old Lawrence place and fix it up as a bed and breakfast.

Mama: Heavens to Murgatroyd! That place is falling apart.

Bertha: I heard tell she's got tons of money and friends in the television business. She's talking to them about making a tv show of them restoring the property and then opening up the B and B.

Mama: Well, if that don't beat all! Right here in Diggsville.

I hope you get the drift. Mama used these phrases as I would use the much less colorful "Wow!" or "Really?" or "Good grief." Surprise in the form of excitement, wonder, disbelief, or disappointment.

Let's talk about "If that don't beat all." It is another way of saying, "That is more surprising than all other surprising facts and occurrences. It wins the contest of surprising things."

Think for a moment about surprising things recounted in Scripture:

- The creation of the universe (Genesis 1)

- Sarah having a baby at age 90 (Genesis 21)

- The parting of the Red Sea (Exodus 14)

- The walls of Jericho falling down (Joshua 6)

- The fire coming down on Mt. Carmel (1Kings 18)

- The three men not burning up in the fiery furnace (Daniel 3)

- Daniel not being eaten in the lions' den (Daniel 6)

- A woman who had bled for 12 years suddenly being healed (Luke 8)

- Lazarus being raised from the dead (Luke 11)

I could go on. I'm sure you thought of others as you were recalling these. But even more surprising than these miracles, which are quite astonishing, is this: God loves us and gave His only Son to die for us.

> I look up at your macro-skies, dark and enormous,
>   your handmade sky-jewelry,
> Moon and stars mounted in their settings.
>   Then I look at my micro-self and wonder,
> Why do you bother with us?
>   Why take a second look our way?
> (Psalm 8:3-4, The Message)

How priceless is your unfailing love, O God!
    People take refuge in the shadow of your wings.
They feast on the abundance of your house;
    you give them drink from your river of delights.
For with you is the fountain of life;
    in your light we see light. (Psalm 36:7-10)

The Lord is compassionate and gracious,
    slow to anger, abounding in love.
He will not always accuse,
    nor will he harbor his anger forever;
he does not treat us as our sins deserve
    or repay us according to our iniquities.
For as high as the heavens are above the earth,
    so great is his love for those who fear him;
as far as the east is from the west,
    so far has he removed our transgressions from us.

As a father has compassion on his children,
    so the Lord has compassion on those who fear him;
for he knows how we are formed,
    he remembers that we are dust.
The life of mortals is like grass,
    they flourish like a flower of the field;
the wind blows over it and it is gone,
    and its place remembers it no more.
But from everlasting to everlasting
    the Lord's love is with those who fear him,
    and his righteousness with their children's children.
(Psalm 103:8-17)

The Lord appeared to us in the past, saying:
"I have loved you with an everlasting love;
    I have drawn you with unfailing kindness. (Jeremiah 31:3)

Because of his great love for us, God, who is rich in mercy, made us alive with Christ even when we were dead in transgressions—it is by grace you have been saved.
(Ephesians 2:4-5)

I pray that you, being rooted and established in love, may have power, together with all the Lord's holy people, to grasp how wide and long and high and deep is the love of Christ, and to know this love that surpasses knowledge—that you may be filled to the measure of all the fullness of God.
(Ephesians 3:17-19)

In this last passage, Paul was stressing that believers need to understand the surprising and generous love of God. First, he said to be rooted and grounded in God's love. Being rooted means to receive nourishment and life from it, and being grounded means to get stability from it. Some plants have flimsy, shallow roots and can be easily jerked out of the ground and destroyed. Others have deep, strong roots. The plant itself might be jerked off and destroyed, but the root remains. Our roots need to be deep and strong in God's love. We need to be certain of it and assured in it. According to Paul, we do this by knowing the dimensions of the knowledge-surpassing love of Christ. "Knowledge-surpassing" means you can't know it. The paradox here is that we need to know what surpasses human knowledge. The only way we can do this is by humbling ourselves to the Holy Spirit in us.

What are the dimensions of God's love?

Breadth (How wide is it?)

John 3:16 – God so loved <u>the world</u>

John 10:9 – "I am the gate; <u>whoever</u> enters through me will be saved."

Matthew 11:28 – "Come to me <u>all</u> who are weary and burdened, and I will give you rest."

Isa. 55:1 – "Ho! <u>Everyone</u> who thirsts, come to the waters." (NKJV)

Rev. 3:20 – "Behold, I stand at the door and knock. If <u>anyone</u> hears My voice and opens the door, I will come in to him and dine with   him, and he with Me." (NKJV)

Length (How long does it last?)

Bible scholar Vernon McGee says, "It begins with the Lamb slain before the foundation of the world and proceeds unto the endless ages of eternity."

1 John 4:16 – God *is* love (present tense forever and ever)

Jer. 31:3 – He loves with an *everlasting* love.

Ps. 136:26 – His love endures *forever.*

Depth (How deep is it?)

Phil. 2:8 – He became obedient to death – even death on a cross.

Rom. 8:38-39 – Nothing can tear us up out of the soil of His love.

- No angel or demon
- Not the present or the future
- No power
- Nothing in all creation

Height (How high is it?)

It reaches and brings us to the throne of God.

I hope that as you've read this book and when you read your Bible you truly understand that God's love beats all and that He wants you. He wants to have a relationship with you. He wants to give you purpose. He wants you to experience his joy and peace. Give your heart and life to him now. His love beats all.

*I'm pretty sure Mama got this recipe from me, but I didn't invent it. It definitely "beats all" the slaw-type salads I've ever tasted.

Broccoli Salad

<u>Dressing</u>:

½ cup sugar

1 cup mayonnaise

2 T. red wine or apple cider vinegar

2 bunches of broccoli, washed, trimmed, and chopped

½ cup chopped scallions OR ½ large purple onion, thinly sliced

½ cup raisins

½ cup sunflower seeds

8 slices bacon, cooked and crumbled

Mix dressing ingredients together and set aside. Mix all dry ingredients except bacon. Add dressing and stir well. Refrigerate overnight. Add the bacon right before serving.

Made in the USA
Middletown, DE
06 January 2021